"This book is an invitation to a homecoming—a clear, simple, yet incredibly powerful concept that should not be lightly dismissed by any of us. Worship is the place God has always desired us to be in relation to Himself, and for many of us this will require renewal and restoration. *Return to Worship* points the way."

Rob Hewell
Team Leader, Leadership & Worship Team, Arkansas Baptist State Convention
President, Southern Baptist Church Music Conference

"With the wisdom and skill that can come only from wide experience, serious study, and sincere devotion to Christ and His Church, Ron Owens gives us the counsel we need in this troubled hour. I wish every believer, church musician, and worship leader would read this book and take it to heart. It calls us back to God-centered worship that is based on truth, not trends, and that brings glory to the Master, not applause to the servants."

Warren W. Wiersbe
Author and Conference Speaker

RETURN TO WORSHIP

A GOD-CENTERED
APPROACH

RETURN TO WORSHIP

A GOD-CENTERED APPROACH

RON OWENS
with Jan McMurray

BROADMAN
& HOLMAN
PUBLISHERS

Nashville, Tennessee

0-8054-1888-1

Published by Broadman & Holman Publishers, Nashville, Tennessee
Editorial Team: Leonard G. Goss, John Landers, Sandra Bryer
Page Design and Typesetting: PerfecType, Nashville, Tennessee

Dewey Decimal Classification: 264
Subject Heading: WORSHIP

Unless otherwise noted, Scripture quotations are from the New King James Version,
copyright © 1979, 1980, 1982, Thomas Nelson, Inc., Publishers.
Passages marked NIV are from the Holy Bible, New International Version, © copyright 1973, 1978, 1984.
Passages marked AMP are from AMP, The Amplified Bible, Old Testament
copyright © 1962, 1964 by Zondervan Publishing House, used by permission,
and the New Testament © The Lockman Foundation 1954, 1958, 1987, used by permission.

Library of Congress Cataloging-in-Publication Data

Owens, Ron.
    Return to worship : a God-centered approach / by Ron Owens : with Jan McMurray.
        p. cm.
    Includes bibliographical references.
    ISBN 0-8054-1888-1 (pbk. : alk. paper)
    1. Public worship. 2. Evangelicalism. 3. Public worship--
Biblical teaching. I. McMurray, Jan. 1955-   . II. Title.
BV15.094   1999
264—dc21
                                                            99–20606
                                                            CIP

13 14 15 16 17 09 08 07 06 05

Dedication

To Patricia, God's "miracle" gift to me, without whom there
would not have been a ministry, let alone a book;

and to Jeff and Jessica, our son and daughter-in-law
whom we love dearly.

Contents

Foreword

I have often been asked what I felt was the most significant factor in God's consistent blessing of His people. I would always answer in one word: worship. As a pastor for almost thirty years, I sought most earnestly to be an authentic worshiper myself and taught God's people to worship as their first response to God.

To know God is to worship God; therefore our view of God will directly affect how we approach Him. In *Return to Worship*, Ron Owens attempts to lead God's people to see that the primary issue to be considered is not the "how" of worship, but rather the "Who" of worship. Who we see God to be will dictate how we approach Him. Much of the North American evangelical church worships a "lesser" God than the God Scripture reveals. If we were to spend less time debating which worship styles were best and more time getting to know God through His Word, we would be worshiping Him more acceptably. To worship God acceptably should be our goal. The sphere of our worship, however, must involve more than worshiping in church; it will involve the whole of our lives, twenty-four hours a day. As the apostle Paul urged the believers in Rome:

> I beseech you, therefore, brethren, by the mercies of God, that
> you present your bodies a living sacrifice, holy, acceptable to God,
> which is your reasonable service [acceptable worship]. And do
> not be conformed to this world, but be transformed by the
> renewing of your mind, that you may prove what is that good
> and acceptable and perfect will of God.
>
> Romans 12:1–2

Ron Owens and I have been colaborers for a number of years. On many occasions, both privately and publicly, we have earnestly attempted to adequately honor God in worship. This written work is the culmination of Ron's lifelong desire to help God's people experience Him deeply in true worship. I feel that this book very fairly and thoroughly addresses the issues God's people are facing today in this area. It is a very exciting and timely contribution to the whole field of worship and will be helpful to those who take worship seriously.

Henry T. Blackaby

Foreword

A. W. Tozer asserted that "worship is the missing Jewel in the Evangelical Church." If that was true in his day, what shall we say of the life of the church in this critical hour of human history?

Someone who shares this profound concern is the author of this book, *Return to Worship*. The Reverend Ron Owens is a man of God, a preacher of the Word, a composer of hymns, a talented soloist, and, supremely, a leader of worship. He and his wife, Patricia, an accomplished pianist, have served the Lord around the world. Their abilities to lead God's people to express in worship, in "awesome wonder and overpowering love," is a constant blessing to me and always a compelling motivation to praise our triune God.

The format that Ron has chosen for the writing of this book is both creative and challenging. It is creative in that it is unusual but not unprecedented. Like the apostle Paul and his contemporaries, Ron's chapters are "Letters to the Churches" dealing with specific issues relating to worship. The approach is not only creative but challenging. Church members are challenged with instructive truth, while church leaders are challenged with corrective tact! Before you disagree with anything that is written, weigh every word in the presence of God with an open Bible and on bended knees.

The purpose for this book is to call God's people back to true worship. So many of us are like the woman of Samaria. Jesus had to say to us: "You worship what you do not know." Then He added one of the greatest sayings ever uttered on earth: "God is Spirit, and those who worship Him must worship in spirit and truth" (John 4:22, 24). In essence, He insisted that we cannot worship until we live in the power of the ungrieved, unquenched Spirit and are willing to conform ourselves to absolute truth. Taken seriously and understood correctly, these words could revolutionize the religious thinking, living, and serving of evangelicals today. Jesus tells us that "the Father is seeking [present tense] such [as we are] to worship Him" (John 4:23). What a mind-boggling concept—the Father is *seeking* us! He seeks us in our totality. He wants our spirits in adoration; He wants our souls in contemplation; He wants our bodies in dedication; He wants our service in consecration. This is Christ in worship.

In New Testament times, Christian worship consisted of and included the preaching of the Word (Acts 20:7; 1 Cor. 14:19), the reading of Scripture (James 1:22; Col. 4:16), the offering of prayers (1 Cor. 14:14–16; 1 Tim. 2:1–5), the singing of praises (Eph. 5:19; Col. 3:16), the ordinances of baptism and the Lord's Supper (Acts 2:41; 1 Cor. 11:18–34), the offering of gifts (1 Cor. 16:1–2), and most importantly, the dedication of lives to do God's good, acceptable, and perfect will (Rom. 12:1–2). Calvin Coolidge once observed: "It is only when men begin to worship that they begin to grow."

Return to Worship is the precursor to heaven-sent revival, spiritual awakening, and worldwide evangelization. I commend this book to church members and leaders everywhere—with the fervent prayer that God will use it to bring us back to the highest activity of which a redeemed person is capable, namely, the worship of God in spirit and in truth.

> Stephen F. Olford
> Founder of the Stephen Olford Center for Biblical Preaching
> Memphis, Tennessee

Preface

I have always found it easier to express myself when writing a letter. I recall how, during my teenage years, I would climb the mountain behind my family's hotel in Switzerland, presumably to study. But when I reached my favorite spot, I would more often dream and write. The only sounds to invade the awesome silence were cowbells from a nearby pasture and the occasional "shush" of a bird's wings as it flew by.

The letters I wrote from that place high above the noise of life were sometimes to a Sunday School teacher in Canada, where I had lived until I was fourteen. He had taken time to be more than just a teacher of young boys; he had been a friend. My letters to him were never mailed because I did not have his address. It was good, however, to be able to express myself in that way. Sometimes I wrote letters to the Lord. I never mailed them either. I knew, though, that He read them, as He had read the others.

I wrote about the good and the bad of life during those years. I wrote about my frustrations, the exciting experiences, the changes that were taking place in me. I even wrote about the embarrassing moments. I asked a lot of questions in those letters, and as I wrote, I seemed to get some answers. Those were very private times, and I suppose they were therapeutic. I wish I still had the letters, but unfortunately they were lost. When I came to the States to go to college in 1956, I put them in a satchel, along with the money I was carrying with me onboard ship. The satchel was stolen. It's funny; at the time I thought only of the money. Now, I wish I had the letters.

I have returned to this way of expression for this book. It is nothing new, for this form of communication was used extensively in Scripture. In fact, most of the New Testament is made up of letters. The last message the Lord gave directly to the early church was given in the form of letters dictated through the beloved apostle John.

Though I have deep convictions on the subject of worship, convictions which I believe are grounded in Scripture, I am also writing as one who seeks to know the truth. I feel as though I am just a learner. There are those who have been labeled "experts" in the field of worship, but I am not one of them. Nor do I want to be. In fact, I wonder how anyone could be an expert on something as profound as worship. To say you know everything about worship is to say you know everything about God. I don't and never will. Seeking to understand true worship has been a lifelong quest and will continue to be so, I expect, throughout eternity.

In his first letter, the apostle John expressed his deep love and concern for the "children of God" and gave warnings against those who would deceive them. He used the phrase "I write to you" repeatedly in the second chapter as he wrote to specific groups and gave his purpose for writing them.

The letters in this book, too, have grown out of a heart of love and concern for the present-day church. Some of them are written to the church as a whole, some to specific groups, and some to individuals. Questions are raised, problems are addressed, instruction is offered, and sometimes warnings are given. All the letters are written with the hope that we will come to a fuller understanding of what worship is and fulfill in a more excellent way the highest call that is placed on the believer's life: to offer Almighty God acceptable worship.

And so, I begin. "Dear Church, I write to you . . . ."

Ron Owens

Acknowledgments

To acknowledge all those whose lives have contributed to whatever insight the Lord has given me on the subject of this book would take many pages. The names I mention here are but a few to whom I owe so much.

My wife, Patricia, who patiently and lovingly walked with me over these last several years of "on-again, off-again" writing; encouraging, listening, reading, suggesting.

My mother and father, John and Hazel Owens, who faithfully modeled a reverence for God in worship that is so often missing in our day.

E. A. Frink, who, during a time of major crisis in my life, was used of the Lord to help me make the "right choice."

John L. Fain Jr., of the Presbyterian Evangelistic Fellowship, who early in our ministry was used to lead us to a new love for God's Word and to an understanding of the primacy of the preaching of God's Word in worship.

Joe Ann Shelton, our friend, encourager, faithful prayer partner, listener, and counselor, with whom we have walked over many miles.

Manley Beasley, who confirmed our conviction that there is a difference between soulish and spiritual music.

Stephen F. Olford, who over the years has always pointed us to the glory and magnificence of God and was the first to encourage us not only to model worship but also to teach about it.

Henry Blackaby, with whom we have been privileged to be partnered in ministry for these last years and who has been greatly used of the Lord in our lives, has been a constant encourager to us to finish this book. Thank you, Henry.

✳

Jan McMurray, without whom this book might never have made it to the publisher, whose labor of love and insights were a gift from God.

All the "unknown" ones from whom I have learned over the years, to which the myriad of notes attest. And most especially to whoever it was who opened my eyes to a fresh new understanding of the Commandments, the source of which I have been unable to trace.

Among the most humbling moments in life is when someone tells you that they "never cease praying for you." To all of you who over the years have been faithfully "holding the ropes"—thank you!

PART 1

Letters to the Church

———◆———

Defining Worship Biblically

◆

The most important and highest activity that a company of God's people could ever engage in, is to offer Almighty God acceptable worship.
—*D. Martyn Lloyd-Jones*

DEAR CHURCH,

It seems that everyone in the church today is talking about worship. Some promote one kind and some another, usually with each side claiming his is preferable. With so much confusion and division occurring because of this issue of worship, the only safe place to go for answers is to the Bible. Contrary to what some say, Scripture does clearly define what true worship is.

Often when people think of worship, their minds immediately turn to music. They think of music styles and talk of the type of "worship" or music they "like." To them, worship is seen only in the context of music. When I ask people about the worship in their church, they usually respond with something like "we have contemporary worship" or "our worship is traditional" or "we have blended services." All of these responses describe the kind of music they have. This raises a foundational question we must answer if we are really serious about worshiping God acceptably: What does Scripture teach us about worship?

The first words we read in the Bible are, "In the beginning God created." These words are echoed in the first words of John's Gospel: "In the beginning was the Word." I don't believe we violate Scripture by also saying that "in the beginning was worship."

We know that worship played a major role in heaven's activity in eternity past. It was during this time that the sin of pride entered into Lucifer's heart, and he became jealous of God. He wanted to be the one who received heaven's adoration. He wanted all of heaven, including God, to bow down to him. He wanted to be the one in charge, and this led to the organizing of the universe's first rebellion. There was mutiny in heaven, and it was over worship.

Lucifer and his followers were cast out of heaven, but the effort to unseat God from His throne was not over. This was never so clear as when, following His baptism by John the Baptist, our Lord was led by the Spirit into the wilderness to be tempted by the devil. At the heart of this encounter with Satan was the issue of worship. "All these things I will give You if You will fall down and worship me," said Satan to the Son of God (Matt. 4:9).

To this day, conflict rages in the human heart over who will ultimately be worshiped. Whom will those who have been created in God's image worship? Before whom will the heavens and the earth bow? The real issue in worship is not *if* we will worship or *how* we will worship, but *whom* we will worship. Everyone worships someone or something, for worship is built into the very fiber of God's creation. Those who visit even the most remote, primitive tribes find people worshiping something. Missionaries have long recognized this fact. Their work involves not so much convincing the natives of the existence of God as the conversion of the people's hearts from allegiance to their gods to the worship of the One True God.

This was what the apostle Paul faced in Athens. "Men of Athens, I perceive that in all things you are very religious; for as I was passing through and considering the objects of your worship, I even found an altar with this inscription: TO THE UNKNOWN GOD" (Acts 17:22–23). Sometimes you find a mixture of religions. It is not uncommon to find polytheism, which is the worship of more than one god. But no matter what or who it is, people worship.

Since we have all been created to worship God, it is therefore of fundamental importance to understand what He had in mind when He created us. Although we may not be polytheistic in our worship today, we certainly have numerous ideas of what worship is. I have no doubt that the enemy is using this misunderstanding to confuse God's people.

A major part of the problem we face in understanding *worship* is that the word *worship*, like many other words in our vocabulary, has lost much of its original meaning. Unlike other words in our culture that may evolve, the meaning that God attaches to a word establishes it once and for all, for *God does not change.* We do change, and we often redefine the things of God in order to fit them into our way of thinking at the moment. This has happened with our understanding of worship.

What we think, however, does not change what God has established. God does not adjust to us; we must adjust to Him. We must return to Him or suffer the consequences of departing. We are in need today of *returning* to the practice of scriptural worship. "'Return to Me,' says the LORD of hosts, 'and I will return to you'" (Zech. 1:3).

So what does God have to say about worship in Scripture? How does He define the word, and what does He require? When the word *worship* is found in Scripture, it means essentially the same thing in both the Old and New Testaments. In the Old Testament, two words are predominantly used: *shachah,* and *abad. Abad* connotes the idea of work, bond-service, labor, or general service, which is a form of worship. The aspect of worship I want to focus on in these letters, however, is that described by the word, *shachah,* a word found often in the Old Testament and meaning to prostrate oneself, to bow down or stoop before the one you are worshiping. In the New Testament the primary word used for worship is *proskuneo* and means essentially the same thing: to crouch, to prostrate oneself in homage, to reverence and adore, with the added picture of "kissing the hand."

Those of us who grew up under a monarchy can perhaps relate better to the practice of bowing and doing homage than those who live in the United States. Though we (I am now an American citizen) are usually respectful to those over us, we don't call our president "Your Highness" or our judges "Your Worship." Yet that is the exact attitude of heart found in this word *worship.* The accepted protocol is to bow or even kneel. Throughout the Old Testament we find people bowing in worship. Young David bowed before King Saul. In Joseph's dream, he saw his brothers' sheaves bowing down before his sheaf. There are times when the word *shachah* is used in conjunction with another Hebrew verb for bowing down physically, followed by the word *worship.* "Moses . . . bowed his head toward the earth, and worshiped" (Exod. 34:8). According to Scripture, then, worship must necessarily involve a bowing, specifically a bowing of the heart before our God.

As wonderful and important as music is, the truth is we don't have to have music to worship. In fact, we have no record of music during much of the private or corporate worship recorded in Scripture. Music can be and often is a part of worship, but it is not fundamentally necessary. It is my conviction that in much of the Western Church today, music has become overly impor- tant. *To many, worship is music, and music is worship, and many worship music.*

What, then, are the things that are fundamental to worship? What are the essentials in offering God acceptable worship? We won't find them in human reasoning, for that is nothing but man's opinion and is what has created the division over worship in the church in the first place. The only safe and sure place to turn is to the Scriptures. What does God say in His Word, by direct instruction and through examples, that will help us understand what worship really is? God established some basic principles in this regard, and only by looking at what He said to His people in the beginning, as He established them as a nation, as He laid down guidelines for their living and standards for their worship, can we understand true worship.

As I write these letters to you, my brothers and sisters in Christ, I pray that we can all come to a deeper understanding of what worship truly is from God's perspective.

Our View of God

We've humanized God, deified man, and minimized sin.
—Bishop John R. Moore

DEAR CHURCH,

I wonder how often we, as Christians, stop to think about how we view our God and how our view of Him affects our ability to worship. Sometimes it seems we have completely lost sight of Who God is—His might, His majesty, His justice, His mercy, His Holiness. Instead, we seem to imagine Him as being on our level, yet nothing could be further from the truth.

I see this attitude reflected in the church today. In reality, many of the popular Christian songs being sung seriously misrepresent God. The emphasis on Christ's humanity in our song literature is far out of proportion to His deity. Somehow we've managed to conceive of a god who is "one of us." I once heard a song on Christian radio that had this recurring phrase: "He's just like me." This kind of thinking is close to blasphemy. I thank my God that He's not like me! Although our Savior stooped to become a man, to put on flesh and live among us, He never ceased being God. He lived a sinless life and offered Himself in sacrifice "for someone just like me," but He was never "just like me."

It's not surprising that the world should attempt to bring God down to its level. But we cannot allow the tendency to do so to go unchallenged when it occurs within the church. We, of all people, must develop and project a correct image of God, to one another as well as to the world. Fundamental to offering God acceptable worship is having a correct view of who He is. If our view of God is anything other than His Self-revelation through His Word, then the god we worship is one of our own making, one fashioned to suit what we want God to be.

A magnificent picture of the apostle Paul's view of God is found in 1 Timothy 1:17, as he writes his first letter to his son in the ministry: "Now to the King eternal, immortal, invisible, to God who alone is wise, be honor and glory forever and ever. Amen." Every letter Paul wrote, every prayer he prayed, every sermon he preached was shaped by his view of God. It never wavered. The God he served was the God who had provided a lamb for Abraham on Mount Moriah. This was the God Jacob encountered in a night of wrestling; afterward he bore a limp and a new name for the rest of his life. This was the God who revealed Himself to Moses at the burning bush, who delivered His people from Egyptian slavery, and who declared to them at Mount Sinai that He was the *only* God. They were never to bow down and worship any other.

This was the God Saul of Tarsus met on his way to Damascus, an encounter that would instantaneously change the church's most ardent persecutor into the New Testament's greatest missionary. The apostle Paul's uncompromising dedication to the One "who alone is wise" was shaped by his view of God. This view was that the immortal, invisible God had come to earth; He had disclosed who He was in the form of man; and this disclosure was made in His only Son, Jesus Christ. For the rest of Paul's life, he lived in absolute awe that in Christ God had revealed the perfect picture of who He was. Somehow we seem to have lost sight of this, and its loss has deeply affected our ability to worship.

The worship of the New Testament believers was always through Christ, in Christ, and for Christ. The same must be true for us today. The work of the Holy Spirit is to keep our eyes on the Lord because our very living, and therefore our worship, is to be "of Him and through Him and to Him" (Rom. 11:36). As long as we keep that focus, we will stay on track. The moment we step beyond the boundaries of God's Word, however, we are in danger of forming opinions about God that fit our own personal experiences or lifestyle.

There is so much emphasis today in the evangelical church on experiences. If an experience a person has had is perceived as having done him some good, then the experience is acceptable, even though it may contradict Scripture's view of God's character. Some time ago, a minister acquaintance endorsed a certain movement because during a visit to the location where this movement began his cholesterol had dropped significantly. In the endorsement, however, he had to overlook some questionable things that were taking place, things that were contrary to the Bible's description of our awesome, majestic God.

We live in a day when this seeking after experiences is as much a part of the life of the evangelical as the New Ager. We too are often guilty of trying to adapt God to our ways rather than our adapting to His. Our concept of God is sure to be faulty when He is conceived out of our emotions, preconceived notions, or what makes us feel good, rather than out of His Word. This probably happens more in the area of music than any other because of its powerful influence on our emotions. This is very dangerous, for just because something makes us feel good does not necessarily make it right. Our highest thoughts, arrived at apart from the truth of God's Word, can mount no higher than our emotions or natural mind can reach. When this happens, we don't really see God, for our thoughts are not His thoughts nor our ways His ways. Instead, we see something created by our imagination or experiences.

In a secular world that is constantly vying for our thought life, in a Christian world that often interprets who God is by experiences and thinks it needs to bring God down closer to man's level in order to make Him more accessible, it is vital that we continuously think of, and on, the excellency and majesty of God. When we do, we will be driven to the depth of worship that Job, Isaiah, and Habakkuk reached. Then we, too, will bow in dust and ashes before the awesome, holy God of glory.

The psalmist said in Psalm 104, "O Lord my God, You are very great: You are clothed with honor and majesty" (v. 1). The apostle Paul instructed the believers to think on whatever was noble, right, pure, lovely, admirable, excellent, and praiseworthy (Phil. 4:8, paraphrased). The Puritans used to say, "Think greatly of the greatness of God."

I think this is one of the roots of the problem we are facing in our worship. We don't know our God. The measure in which we know God is the measure in which we will be able to worship Him. And the means by which we get to know God is through His Word. In Scripture we have the revelation of God's nature—His acts and His ways.

Donald W. McCullough once wrote an article that appeared in *Intercessors for America Newsletter* (June 1996). In it he depicted the vital connection between our view of God and our ability to offer true worship: "The New

Testament warns us, 'Offer to God an acceptable worship with reverence and awe; for indeed our God is a consuming fire'. (Heb. 12:28–29). But reverence and awe have often been replaced by a yawn of familiarity. The consuming fire has been domesticated into a candle flame, adding a bit of religious atmosphere, perhaps, but no heat, no blinding light, no power for purification. When the true story gets told, whether in the partial light of historical perspective or in the perfect light of eternity, it may well be revealed that the worst sin of the Church at the end of the twentieth century has been the trivialization of God."

It may not be an exaggeration to say that most people know God today for what He does for them rather than for who He is. That was the basic difference between Israel's knowledge of God and Moses' knowledge of Him. Israel knew God's acts, but Moses knew His ways. If we are going to be worshipers who delight the heart of God, we must become so by understanding His ways and by loving Him for who He is, not just for what He does for us.

The Franciscan monk Brother Lawrence was one who had an intense love for God. He deeply desired to serve God without any reward for himself. One day he expressed the wish that he could do just one thing for God in such a way that God would not know he had done it. So deep was his love that he wanted to do something for God for which he would not be rewarded or blessed in return.

What a contrast this attitude is to the prevailing attitude of today. How many would be in church if they were not offered all the free benefits that come with membership? What if getting to know God was all the benefit there was to belonging to a church? Would that be enough for us?

On his deathbed, Brother Lawrence woke from a coma and startled those who were attending him by saying, "I am not dying!" His friends and fellow monks asked him, "Then what are you doing, Brother Lawrence?" He replied, "I am doing what I have been doing all my life. I am worshiping the God I love."

Our capacity to understand God may be limited, because now we can only see through a glass darkly. Nevertheless, we can see. Through God's Self-revelation in His Word and the Holy Spirit, our Teacher, we can grow in the knowledge of God. We must grow. We must know who God is if we are going to worship Him as He desires.

LETTER 3

God's Plumb Line
for Worship

◆

*The only standard, or plumb line, that stretches unchanged throughout history is the standard
of God's Word. In it we have the revelation of God's character, who He is,
and what He requires. There is no other goodness or rightness apart from Him.*

DEAR CHURCH,

Every time you turn around, it seems someone is setting a new record or
proposing new standards. Things are constantly in flux. What is a given today
will be changed tomorrow. What should concern us is that this changing of
standards is not limited to things like the environment or automobile safety. It
has now entered the arena of morality, and the changes are happening more
quickly here than in any other arena of life. And it is very obvious that when
moral standards change, they never are raised. They are always lowered.

As I write this letter, some political leaders in our nation, who call themselves "Christian," are showing a blatant disregard for what Scripture says
about the very things they have been condoning and even promoting. I recall
a speech Senator Patrick Moynihan gave several years ago in which he talked
about "defining deviancy down." He pointed out how we are adjusting our
moral code and standards to match the decline of morality in our country.
This way we can continue to think well of ourselves because we are meeting
our own standards. Yet with every new standard we set, we move farther away
from God.

As shocking as it is to think our nation is actually doing this, it is even
more shocking to find the church, which is supposed to be setting the standard,

actually contributing to the decline. And this inclination to reinterpret what God has said, in order for it to fit how we want to live, has entered every part of our lives as Christians. It is even affecting how the church views worship.

The standard God set thousands of years ago is as relevant today as it was when Moses carried the tablets down from the mountain. The Ten Commandments were the basis of the Old Testament law. The first four deal with our relationship to God. They address His fundamental requirements for worship. The last six commandments deal with our relationship to other people. The commandments are the basis of God's standard of living for His people. If our desire is to please and honor Him, we will obey what He has told us to do. If we want to offer Him acceptable worship, we will heed what He says about worship. As we obey these commands, we personify to the world, in our living and in our worshiping, what God is like, for behind each of the commandments stands God. The commandments reveal His character. First Peter 1:15–16 gives us this instruction: "But as He who called you is holy, you also be holy in all your conduct, because it is written, 'Be holy, for I am holy.'"

God did not give these commandments to restrict us but to liberate us. I believe this is where a lot of people are confused. Most people think of the commandments as restrictive, but they were given to free us to be all that God created us to be. To me, that is an incredible thought. When we consider the commandments to be negative or restrictive, we are misunderstanding God's purpose for giving them in the first place. The reason there is such a battle going on in our land over whether they should even be hung in government buildings is because the world doesn't understand their purpose. They can only see them as being restrictive, because they have not yet been delivered out of bondage to sin. What really is sad, however, is when Christians see the commandments in that light.

Have you thought about the significance of the order of events in the life of God's people, Israel? The commandments were given to them after their deliverance from bondage, not before. They were not given so the people could earn their freedom in any way; their freedom was not something that could be earned. All their freedom came from grace.

Do you see the significance of this? If their salvation, or freedom from bondage, could have been earned, God would have said to Moses at the burning bush, "I am going to give you a list of rules that you are to take to My people in Egypt. You are to tell them that if they carefully observe all that I tell them to do, I will come and free them from Egyptian slavery." We know He didn't say that, yet there are millions of people in the world today who feel and act that way. They think their salvation must or can be earned. They think that their getting to heaven one day depends on their works.

But God didn't say that to Moses. He said, "I am the God of your father—the God of Abraham, the God of Isaac, and the God of Jacob. . . . I have surely seen the oppression of My people who are in Egypt, and have heard their cry. . . . So I have come down to deliver them out of the hand of the Egyptians, and to bring them up from that land to a good and large land, to a land flowing with milk and honey" (Exod. 3:6–8).

"I have come down to rescue them," God told his people. "I am the Lord your God, who brought you out of Egypt, out of the land of slavery." They were free, free at last! Now He would give them His guidelines for living in that freedom. Do you see why it is important that we understand the reason the commandments were given, and that therefore they are just as relevant today as they were the day they were delivered? "He has delivered us from the power of darkness and conveyed us into the kingdom of the Son of His love, in whom we have redemption through His blood, the forgiveness of sins" (Col. 1:13–14). There is no way we can earn salvation. It is God's free gift. It is His divine favor. It is all His grace!

Although it is not in any of the hymnals these days, there is a song we used to sing years ago that expresses what I am trying to say.

> Grace, 'tis a charming sound, harmonious to the ear;
> Heaven with the echo shall resound, and all the earth shall hear.
> Saved by grace alone, this is all my plea,
> Jesus died for all mankind, and Jesus died for me!

By now you may be wondering what all of this has to do with worship. It has everything to do with it, because it is here that worship begins. Just as Psalm 24:3–4 says, "Who may ascend into the hill of the Lord? Or who may stand in His holy place? He who has clean hands and a pure heart, Who has not lifted up his soul to an idol, Nor sworn deceitfully," so the commandments are God's timeless standard for us, His people. They are not Old Testament or New Testament; they are God. To disregard any of them and think that our worship will be acceptable to Him is self-deceptive. Though there are ten, I'm only going to be writing to you about the first four, since these deal specifically with our relationship to God. The first two are really the foundation upon which all true worship is built, and the next two directly affect our attitude toward God and thus toward worship.

Before I talk about the commandments, however, I want to look at the verse that precedes them (Exod. 20:2). I can't imagine how God could get any more direct in depicting who He is. His opening statement of self-identification would leave no question in the minds of His people as to Who was speaking: "I am the LORD your God." This is how He introduced Himself. I've noticed this is something God did many times in the Old Testament, especially when He was about to make a covenant with His people or had a word of warning, judgment, or some other important thing to say to them. "I am YAHWEH." He didn't pull any punches in establishing the fact that He is God and He *is their* God. They seemed to be forever forgetting this. This lack of understanding was at the root of all their departures from Him. We have the same problem today, don't we?

The importance of establishing this in our minds as we look at the subject of worship cannot be overemphasized. Much of today's controversy in the area of worship would be resolved if God's people would settle once and for all that God alone is God, that He is the same God who is revealed in the Bible, and that He has not changed. He is just as holy as He ever was. He is just as majestic as He ever was. His standards have not changed. His requirements for approaching Him have not changed. That is why *the fundamental issue today is not the "how" of worship, but it is the "Who" of worship*. It is not styles or tastes that must be our primary concern.

Instead of spending all our time discussing "how" we worship, we need to be asking God to help us *change the way we think about Him*. We need an adjustment in our thinking. We need a reformation that will change the heart of the church and restore a true love for God and His Word. We need a revival that will bring back the fear, awe, and reverence for who He is. Until this happens, we will go on debating and addressing peripheral issues. Church staffs will go on dividing their congregations by musical tastes and holding separate services accordingly. We will go on discussing how we can accommodate the world with our worship, so the world will feel "at home" when they attend our worship services.

In the meantime, however, we as individuals must personally make the adjustments needed in our own hearts so that we will be true worshipers. God may then use us to help restore the kind of corporate worship to our churches we know He desires—the kind of worship that will bring Him glory. We need to begin comparing what we do to the standards of God's Word and stop comparing ourselves to one another. Our view of the *Who* will determine the *how*. Our view of God will directly impact how we approach Him.

Worshiping Other Gods

The heavens will praise Your wonders, O LORD;
Your faithfulness also in the assembly of the saints.
For who in the heavens can be compared to the LORD?
Who among the sons of the mighty can be likened to the LORD?
God is greatly to be feared in the assembly of the saints,
And to be held in reverence by all those around Him.
O LORD God of hosts,
Who is mighty like You, O LORD?
Your faithfulness also surrounds You.
—Psalm 89:5–8

DEAR CHURCH,

Have you ever considered the vital relationship between worship and the commandments given by God to His people? As I have said before, the first four commandments establish God's essential requirements for acceptable worship. If we sincerely desire to understand what true worship is, we must begin by studying these commandments.

The first commandment God gave to the children of Israel established the fact that He was the only God they were to worship. He knew that those in the culture in which they lived would be worshiping others gods, and He made His requirements clear: "You shall not bow down to them nor serve [worship] them. For I, the LORD your God, am a jealous God" (Exod. 20:5).

Throughout the Old Testament, the breaking of the first commandment evoked God's anger against His people more than anything else they did. When this one was broken, the breaking of the next three was soon to follow.

His people would create idols, they would blaspheme His name, and they would begin to desecrate the Sabbath.

"You shall have no other gods before Me" (Exod. 20:3). That's it! In other words, God was saying, "Nothing is to be more important in your life than I am. You are free to worship and love Me with all your heart, soul, mind, and strength. You can go to any means to express this, and in return you will be the recipient of My own love, grace, and provision. Just make sure you remember that *I Am your God.*"

We may think that we no longer have this tendency to worship other gods. Maybe this is because we don't recognize the ones we may be serving. When we think of other gods, we usually think of those who worship Buddha, Mohammed, or the multitude of other deities in our world. Of course we believe there is only one God, and He is the only one we are going to worship. We would never be guilty of worshiping other gods! Yet this first commandment may be the one most often violated by God's people today. Maybe we have turned to the worship of idols without even realizing it.

In Old Testament times, the idols a nation worshiped represented the values and belief system of that nation. Every culture had its religious roots and worshiped someone or something. Its idols were reflected in the way the people lived—what they ate, the music they listened to, and the clothes they wore. As the children of Israel interacted with the nations around them, they often incorporated the gods of those nations into their own worship. In doing so they embraced the values of those nations, whether in part or in whole. They embraced the attitudes and lifestyle of that people. When this happened, God became very angry.

God became angry because by their actions they were profaning everything He was. He had given them clear guidelines concerning how they were to live. When His people embraced the culture and gods of the nations around them, those nations would then receive a totally false impression of who He was and what He was like.

With God, however, there could be no mixture or compromise. Either they worshiped Him exclusively, or they would come under His disciplining hand. The nations would then see, in His judging of His people, that He was a holy God. This was made clear in His words to the prophet Ezekiel: "Therefore say to the house of Israel, 'Thus says the Lord GOD: "I do not do this for your sake, O house of Israel, but for My holy name's sake, which you have profaned among the nations wherever you went. And I will sanctify My great name, which has been profaned among the nations, which you have profaned in their midst; and the nations shall know that I am the LORD," says the Lord GOD, "when I am hallowed in you before their eyes"'" (Ezek. 36:22–23).

Contrast backsliding Israel's actions with the stand taken by Daniel and three other young Hebrew men who found themselves in the middle of a heathen culture. These youths had been carried into exile by Nebuchadnezzar. They had been given Babylonian names and told to eat Babylonian food. Daniel, however, "purposed in his heart that he would not defile himself with the portion of the king's delicacies, nor with the wine which he drank; therefore he requested of the chief of the eunuchs that he might not defile himself" (Dan. 1:8).

You recall that at one point Nebuchadnezzar built an image of gold ninety feet high and sent word throughout the land that when the people heard the music, everyone was to fall down and worship the image. This idol represented everything Babylon stood for. The music represented that heathen culture, and the young Hebrew men knew they could not compromise. They could not bow down to that idol, for in so doing they would renounce their covenant lifestyle which represented the covenant God had made with His people. They would be breaking the commandment not to bow down to any other god. They knew that if they did bow down, they would be accepting and embracing the lifestyle of another god. Their decision was that they would rather die than break covenant with God.

I wonder how many of us have this kind of commitment to worshiping God alone today. The temptation to give in to the idols and lifestyles of the day is and always will be strong. Jesus Himself faced it. He lived in constant conflict with the idols of His day, but He was committed to a lifestyle governed by his relationship with his Father. His lifestyle ran counter to what the gods of Rome stood for. His message ran counter to the teachings of the Jewish powers of His day. The forces of darkness, led by Satan himself, tried to get Him to renounce His commitment to the Father by taking an easier way, but He refused. Eventually all of these forces combined to nail Him to the cross. But through that cross and the resurrection, all the power of all the gods who ever were or ever will be was stripped away.

We as God's people do not have to succumb to the culture and lifestyle of this world. In the power of a victory already won and through the indwelling life of our living Lord, we can live in the world while not being part of it. Yet it seems that many in the church today are embracing the world. Even while professing to serve the Lord, they have become guilty of breaking the first commandment and are serving other gods. They have become like the Israelites, who "feared the LORD, yet served their own gods—according to the rituals of the nations from among whom they were carried away" (2 Kings 17:33). This worship of other gods can be readily seen in their lifestyles.

You see, the lifestyles we choose reflect the god(s) we worship. When we worship Yahweh, our way of living will be consistent with who He is and what He represents. We will find ourselves running counter to the gods and culture of society, as we should, for the religious root of the United States and Canada is no longer the God of the Bible.

If a god represents the heart and soul of a culture, what would be the current god of North America? If we were to build images of the gods of our land, which god would stand the tallest? Before which god would millions of our people be bowing? I believe the answer is obvious: *Mammon*. The god of consumerism. The money god. The god of wealth.

Those who served Mammon in New Testament times were never quite satisfied with what they had. They always wanted more. In worshiping Mammon, they worshiped the god they believed would help them acquire wealth. A culture will worship that which it believes will benefit it the most. When the economy is good, anything goes!

The spirit of Mammon is alive and well today, not only in the world but also in the church. It seems we have forgotten the warning of Jesus: "No one can serve two masters; for either he will hate the one and love the other, or else he will be loyal to the one and despise the other. You cannot serve God and mammon" (Matt. 6:24). This god of consumerism has entered our sanctuaries and sits in our pews. Often it oversees the building of our magnificent church properties and whispers in the ears of those who walk the halls of our evangelical cathedrals: "No longer do you have to say, silver and gold have we none."

Can it really be true that the god of Mammon has been ushered into the church? Each day more churches take on a major financial burden when they go into debt to build larger, more plush buildings, purportedly "for the purpose of ministry." Do we really believe that using such large portions of God's money for paying interest to this world's financial institutions is honoring

Him? Could not that same money be invested in God's kingdom, where it would reap eternal dividends?

I was recently told of a small church in a pioneer area of our country that was in real need of a new building. The little congregation had saved $25,000 in their building fund when they heard of a need for Bibles in an Eastern European country. They asked God what they were to do and ended up sending the entire amount to help meet this need. This sounded foolish to some observers, at least until several months later when the church was notified that the state needed their land for a highway project. In exchange for their present property, the government offered to build a new church for them on another property. This small church's investment in the lives of people they would never meet reaped "an hundredfold" reward. I wonder how often God has wanted to work similar miracles for others in order to bring glory to His name, but because of their lack of faith to do kingdom work His way, He could not. "He [Jesus] did not do many mighty works there because of their unbelief" (Matt. 13:58).

The Bible tells us that our heart will be where our treasure is. Our treasure represents that which causes us to feel most secure and which we believe will be most beneficial to us. The focus of our heart will be the focus of our worship. It would seem that we, as God's church, need to rethink who it is we may be serving.

I was once talking to a pastor friend about this matter of giving for kingdom purposes. His response was, "Ron, our people won't give that kind [large amounts] of money unless it is for something they themselves will benefit from. They have to be able to use the facilities and personally enjoy the programs. Giving that kind of money to something they can't see or won't get some tangible benefit from is another matter."

What a sad commentary on the current heart condition of the church, yet I'm afraid it is true. What is it we are really serving? If what we talk about the most is a reflection of where our heart is, who are we worshiping? Do we talk more about our buildings or about our God?

Should we not ask ourselves personally whether we are buying into our culture's lifestyle by bowing to the god of consumerism? Should we not also be asking whether the god of our culture has persuaded our church to compete with the world's lifestyle? Is there any connection between our no longer having to say, "Silver and gold I do not have," with our no longer experiencing the power of the "What I do have I give you" (Acts 3:6)? It appears that the god of our culture has weakened our testimony, for we are often more quick to testify to the beauty of our buildings than the beauty of our Savior.

It is true that we need a place to meet. It is God's design that we gather to worship, to fellowship, to be equipped to go out and do the work of the ministry. But why, as our meeting places have become more opulent and our programs more costly, are we impacting the world around us less than ever before? Are we worshiping the god of our culture more than we realize? Is the lifestyle of our churches reflecting more the influence of the world than the example of our Savior? The church today is being shaped more by our culture than by the cross.

The issue in the first commandment is one of allegiance and loyalty. What is the ultimate loyalty of your life? For every believer, it should be an unquestioned loyalty and commitment to the living God who delivered us from the slavery of sin and brought us into the freedom of His Son. Such an allegiance to the One who has redeemed us will cause us to reorganize every area of our lives—our actions, work, recreation, social activities, church, and family— around what He tells us to do. It will dictate how we live. The plumb line, or standard, by which we are to measure our lives is the commandments of God. He will stand for no rivals. We cannot serve, we cannot worship both God and the gods of our culture. And we should not be trying. Understanding and applying this truth is fundamental to how and what we worship.

The Imaging of God

The most dangerous thing we can do is to return to spiritual worship.
It would mean the end of the personality cults that have invaded the church.
It would also mean the end of the "Christian consumerism" that has so twisted our sense of
spiritual values. I have no doubt that the church that returned to true worship
would lose people—"important" people—and probably have to make drastic cuts
in the budget. But then—something would happen! A beautiful new sense of
spiritual reality would result, with people glorifying God instead of praising men.
— Warren Wiersbe in Real Worship

DEAR CHURCH,

There is an area in Christian worship today that should cause all of us great concern, yet many seem to be unaware of its significance. It centers on the second commandment, where God said to His people: "You shall not make for yourself a carved image—any likeness of anything that is in heaven above, or that is in the earth beneath, or that is in the water under the earth. . . . For I, the LORD your God, am a jealous God" (Exod. 20:4–5).

When we read this commandment, most of us quickly respond that we are not guilty of carving images and worshiping them. That would be idolatry, unthinkable for a Christian. What we do not realize is that when we fail to project a correct image of God as He has revealed Himself to us in Scripture, we are guilty of creating a false image of God and breaking the second commandment.

God has provided a permanent, complete description of who He is and how He works in His Word. Our understanding of Who He is must result from His revelation of Himself. As His people, the way we represent, or image, Him must be consistent with His Self-revelation in Scripture.

As we follow the pilgrimage of the children of Israel in the Old Testament, we see God expressing various aspects of His nature and giving different pictures of what He is like. He revealed, or imaged, Himself at the foot of Mount Sinai with the cloud and the fire. He imaged His character in the Ten Commandments. He imaged Himself in the ark of the covenant, in which were placed the rod and bread. The seat on top of the ark represented the throne. The ark itself imaged the intimate bond that He had established between Himself and His people, and it was placed in the Holy of Holies where His *shekinah* glory, His presence, dwelt.

Throughout the history of Israel, God was constantly imaging Himself. When Solomon finished praying at the dedication of the temple, God came in fire, and the glory of the Lord filled the place. The actions and words of God are all images of who He is. But when He made His final and complete disclosure of who He was, He made it *in His Son*. "God, who at various times and in various ways spoke in times past to the fathers by the prophets, has in these last days spoken to us by His Son, whom He has appointed heir of all things, through whom also He made the worlds; who being the brightness of His glory and the express image of His person, and upholding all things by the word of His power, when He had Himself purged our sins, sat down at the right hand of the Majesty on high, having become so much better than the angels, as He has by inheritance obtained a more excellent name than they" (Heb. 1:1–4).

The entire Old Testament preimaged the Son. Everything pointed toward Him until, in the fullness of time, He, in whom all the fullness of the Godhead dwelt, would be fleshed out among us. God's primary and complete image of Himself was revealed in Jesus Christ. It is no wonder that God is so jealous of how He is portrayed by His people. No wonder this commandment is so important and significant in His relationship with us.

Even as this commandment was being burned into the stone tablet by God's own hand on the mountain, the Israelites in the valley below were breaking it. They began to get impatient when Moses stayed on the mountain so long. They started to murmur and complain that he had deserted them. They then went to Aaron and asked him to make them a god. So Aaron molded that golden calf from the earrings they brought him, and they declared, "This is your god, O Israel, that brought you out of the land of Egypt!" (Exod. 32:4). The people wanted something they could see. They were not satisfied with a God who only spoke to them; they wanted something more. God became so angry with them that He was about to wipe them out when Moses interceded on their behalf.

In the same way, many today are not content with how God has imaged Himself in His Word. They are not satisfied with a God who does not continuously reveal Himself in some kind of tangible, visible form, so they create an "image" of what they think He may be like. These images, in some cases, become the object of worship and the focus of prayers.

Some Christians seek experiences that do not portray God's character as He has portrayed Himself in Scripture. They are not satisfied with how He has imaged Himself in His Word, so they look for something else. Today people are running all over the world, following phenomenon after phenomenon attributed to God, even though these may be vastly removed from the image He has portrayed in Scripture. They travel far and wide, hoping they too will encounter some unusual, tangible experience of Him. The tragedy is that as soon as they accept anything other than how God has imaged Himself, they open themselves up to deceiving spirits. They no longer use God's plumb line to align their experiences against, and soon just about anything becomes acceptable.

I will never forget how vividly I saw the consequences of this several years ago in the lobby of the Constellation Hotel in Toronto. When I walked in, people were scattered all over the floor. Some were lying on their backs, laughing hysterically. Others were jerking uncontrollably or crawling about on all fours, roaring like lions. Some were lying on their backs, unconscious, having been "slain." Each one of them claimed to be imaging God, yet they were imaging Him in a way He had never imaged Himself. They were not content with God's imaging of Himself; they had to have something more. They were violating the second commandment.

When Israel was divided into two kingdoms, King Jeroboam, in the Northern Kingdom, decided to provide something religious that the two kingdoms could have in common. He set up two places of worship, and it is interesting to note what he used as the common denominator. He put a golden calf in each of the places of worship! These golden calves were not necessarily replacements for God; they were simply manmade images of what man thought God was like. But this was contrary to how God had imaged Himself to them. They were breaking the second commandment, and in the process were giving a false interpretation to the nations around them of what God was really like.

As God's people, we have been given the privilege and responsibility of presenting a correct image of Him to the world. Our chief end is to "glorify God and enjoy Him forever." One of the basic meanings of *to glorify* is to give a correct interpretation of something. This is our calling, yet often we are guilty of projecting a faulty picture of the One we worship.

This is happening today in perhaps unprecedented measure. A simple walk through our Christian bookstores will reveal some of the many ways we are reimaging God. My heart was grieved by what I once read in a newspaper article: "A walk down gift aisles at many Christian stores may turn up tiny, stuffed Bible dolls and 'Jesus is Dino-rific' stuffed dinosaurs. There are pink and chartreuse 'Jesus Loves You' shoelaces. And, perhaps for those awkward moments in the confessional, Testamints breath fresheners ('Come near to God, and He will come near to you')." Are these correct images of our God?

This is not the only way Christians are projecting a faulty image of the God we worship. Watch Christian television and you will find the reimaging of God. Follow some Christian music entertainers and you will see the re-imaging of God. Listen to popular "self-promoting" preachers and you will observe the reimaging of God. Visit the churches that have become theaters and you will participate in the reimaging of God. Watch the Christian soloist who, sensually dressed, reimages God even as she sings about Him. Listen to the preacher tell a joke from the pulpit to get a laugh; he is imaging God. Listen to the church combos that create the atmosphere of a nightclub; they are imaging God. Attend the church pageants where thousands of dollars are spent on theatrics, and you will find people reimaging God.

I wonder if the fundamental reason we have begun to add drama to our worship services could be that we really do not think the preaching of God's Word is sufficient. The inherent danger in man's "imagining" or visually illustrating what Scripture is saying is that he may end up weakening the truth by entertaining the people. This isn't always the case, but it often happens. Although God may use anything or anyone to display His glory, we must never forget that when He chose to image Himself, He did not use drama directors, movie producers, sculptors, or entertainers. He raised up prophets who, empowered by the Holy Spirit, declared to their generation what God was like and then, under the same Holy Spirit's direction, wrote down God's imaging of Himself. No expression of what God is like in Scripture originated in the mind of people. Yet today the church is so full of such "imagining" that it is difficult for the world to know what God is really like.

If we are going to offer God acceptable worship, we have to know who He is. That is why, as I have already said, the Who of worship will dictate how we approach Him. God has imaged Himself completely in His Word and through His Son, Jesus Christ. Jesus said, "He who has seen Me has seen the Father" (John 14:9b). When the revelation of who the Father is in Christ is not enough for us and we fashion something different, we are breaking the second commandment.

It is dangerous not to be satisfied with how God has revealed Himself. Those who nailed our Lord to the cross were those who said they were looking for God, yet they didn't recognize Him. They had devised their own image of how He should be, and the One they saw didn't fit their image!

God has revealed Himself in hundreds of different ways. We are free to express who He is in every one of these. The only restriction God puts on His people is that they are not to create any image of Him that is a distortion of who He is. Today many are saying that the way God has imaged Himself is not adequate for our generation. We hear phrases like "the Bible as it is doesn't speak to this generation. We have to be relevant." What they are really saying is, "We need to reimage God. We need to make Him less severe, perhaps a little less holy. Let's not talk so much about sin, the blood, or the cross. Let's major on love. We need to make the world feel at home in our church services. Our music needs to sound like the music the world is accustomed to listening to. Let's give them what they like. We need to provide an upbeat atmosphere so they will enjoy themselves." And in it all, we are reimaging God.

What would God say? Might His word to us be something like this: "My people, when you gather to worship Me, do it in the nature of how I have revealed Myself to you in Scripture. It doesn't matter if the place where you meet is not aesthetically beautiful. Your pianist doesn't even have to play all the notes, and the choir doesn't have to sing all the harmonies perfectly. It doesn't matter if your group is small. You don't need spotlights, and you don't have to have a state-of-the-art sound system. You don't have to worry about appealing to the world with what you do, because when you worship Me in light of who I am, I will be with you and I will bless you. My people, what matters most is that you worship Me in spirit and in truth. Do not add to or subtract from the truth I have recorded for you in My Word. You don't need anything else to please Me. Just love Me with all your heart. Worship Me; respond to Me as I have imaged Myself to you, and I will use this imaging of Me to draw souls to My Son."

The Use and Misuse of God's Name

The measure in which we know God is the measure in which we will be able to worship Him. The way we get to know God is through the Scriptures. In the Scriptures we have the revelation of God's nature—His ways and who He is.

DEAR CHURCH,

It's quite obvious that we live in an age when the name of God has become essentially meaningless to most people. His name is thrown around as casually as any other word in our language. Yet God made it plain in His third commandment to His people that they were to be careful in the way they used His name: "You shall not take the name of the LORD your God in vain, for the LORD will not hold him guiltless who takes His name in vain" (Exod. 20:7).

You may be wondering how taking God's name in vain relates to the issue of worship. We need to realize that how we use God's name reveals how we really view Him. As I wrote to you before, the way we view God profoundly affects our ability to worship Him acceptably.

Why is the way we use God's name so important to Him? To more fully understand this commandment, we need to learn more about the meaning of names in the Bible.

People in biblical times were quite conscious of the meaning of names. A person's name usually represented that person's character or nature. Remember in Genesis when God told Abram He was going to make his name great? He was about to shape Abram's character to match the assignment He was going to give him. Abram's name was changed to Abraham, "the father of many," and one day he would become the father of many nations. Through his seed, Jesus Christ, all nations would be blessed. Isaiah prophesied that this seed would be called "Wonderful Counselor, Mighty God, Everlasting Father, Prince of Peace" (Isa. 9:6b NIV). In addition to these names, there are literally hundreds of others in the Bible that describe Jesus, each portraying an aspect of His character, or as the Puritans expressed it, each one "a perfection of who He is."

The reputation of a person's name always rests on how he acts or what he does with his life. This is true for all of us. We identify a name with a person we have known, and when we meet another with the same name, an immediate association is made. When a child to whom you have given your name shames it, the name is never quite the same.

This was the complaint God had with His people—the children of Israel, the people to whom He had given His great name. These people were forever profaning it, yet they were His people. They represented who He was. They were called to present an image to the nations around them of what He was like. Israel bore God's name, just as Christians do today.

God's primary reason for still insisting on obedience from His children is concern for His name. In Ezekiel 36:20–23 we read: "When they came to the nations, wherever they went, they profaned My holy name—when they said of them, 'These are the people of the LORD, and yet they have gone out of His land.' But I had concern for My holy name, which the house of Israel had profaned among the nations wherever they went. Therefore say to the house of Israel, 'Thus says the Lord GOD: "I do not do this for your sake, O house of Israel, but for My holy name's sake, which you have profaned among the nations wherever you went. And I will sanctify My great name, which has been profaned among the nations, which you have profaned in their midst; and the nations shall know that I am the LORD," says the Lord GOD, "when I am hallowed in you before their eyes." ' "

God's complaint with His people was that they were misinterpreting to the world what He was like. His name is "Holy," and their lives were anything but holy. God proclaimed that He was going to sanctify His great name which they had profaned. He would do it by bringing severe discipline upon them in front of the nations. In this way, the world would see that He was a holy God.

I write this letter to you as a reminder that giving a correct interpretation of what God is like to the world has always been and is still the calling of God's people. When God gives His name to His people, however, there is the possibility that they will misuse and profane it. When we think of profaning or misusing God's name, our minds immediately go to a situation where some foul-mouthed person could not complete a sentence without inserting God's name in a profanity. This commandment, however, is not limited to those who hold little or no respect for God's name. It applies to any misuse of His name. God wasn't complaining about the heathen nations profaning what was holy; that was expected. His concern, warning, and judgment were directed toward *His own people*. This is particularly significant for us as believers, for we may be more guilty before God than anyone else of misusing His name.

Much of the misuse of God's name among His people does not appear in the form of profanity or other blatant disregard. Instead, it is done in ignorance or lack of awareness. And surprisingly, the time His name is used in vain most frequently is during our worship services. It occurs all too frequently in our preaching, praying, and singing.

When a pastor preaches a message that he is unwilling to apply to his own life, he is guilty of using the name of the Lord lightly. He is breaking the third commandment. We misuse God's name in prayer when we try to manipulate Him to get what we want. We use God's name in vain when we pray prayers that are not scriptural, such as "Lord, if it be Your will, would You be present with us today," as though He might not desire to do so.

We use God's name in vain when we use it to entertain, no matter what the occasion may be. Any use of His name that is not done with respect, in absolute reverence and awe, is a serious breaking of this commandment. In our personal lives, we misuse God's name when we use phrases such as "Praise the Lord" habitually and mean nothing by them. Many times Christians use the words "O God!" as casually as they would use the phrase, "You've got to be kidding!" They don't seem to be aware, or to care, that they are using the name of our Lord in vain.

I believe we have become much too familiar and casual with the things of God, especially with His name. Some time ago I received a letter from a lady who had attended one of my *Return to Worship* seminars. As a teacher of youth in her church, she was concerned over what she had observed at a statewide convention for teenage girls. It seems that the girls had been taught a chorus in which God was described as "a groovy dude who is so cool"! What a message to be passing on to the next generation in the church! That chorus is a reflection of our culture's view of God, not a statement of the biblical view of

God. It is the antithesis of the awe and honor Scripture teaches we are to have for God's name. Those who are in positions of leadership must carefully evaluate what they are teaching, for they will be held accountable for their message.

This kind of message in music isn't new. Disrespect for God and His name has been creeping into the music of the church for years, yet we seem not to notice. After all, the tunes are catchy, the songs are "cute," and we "enjoy" singing them. We fail to consider, however, the image of God they portray and, most of all, how they treat His name.

Over the years we have not only become familiar and casual in the use of the name of God, but we have become disoriented to what it really means to do something *in God's name*. If a name actually does represent the character of the person behind the name, then anything done "in Jesus' name" will have the features of His character. Preaching done in Jesus' name is preaching our Lord Himself could preach or would endorse. A message that He could not preach is a message that should not be preached.

Prayers made in Jesus' name will be prayers our Lord could pray or would say "Amen" to. Often I hear prayers that are neither scriptural nor of faith. To ask God to come and be with us when He has already told us He will be present with any of His children who are meeting "in His name" is to pray in unbelief. To pray, "Lord, if it be Your will, bless us today" is to pray in unbelief. God has made it imminently clear that He wants to bless His children; the problem is that we often are not "blessable." The better prayer might be, "Lord, show us those areas in which we need to repent or make adjustments, so You can bless us." To claim a promise in prayer without being concerned enough to see whether we are meeting the conditions of that promise is to pray in vain and to misuse God's name.

Music played or sung in Jesus' name will be music that our Lord could participate in or would give His full endorsement to. Today we often fall far short of God's standard in this matter. I have heard song lyrics that contradicted what Scripture says, but because the music was enjoyable to the ear and appealed to the senses, little attention was given to the content.

In past generations much, if not most, of the church music was written by ministers—Isaac Watts, John Newton, and Charles Wesley, to name a few. Their texts were scripturally based and theologically sound. Though many good texts are being written today, there is much that lacks either doctrinal integrity or significant meaning. My prayer is that you will be discerning in the music you write or choose for the ministry of your church; may it always be in the character of our Lord's name. After all, it is He whom we are first to please.

Worship offered in Jesus' name will be worship that delights our Lord in every aspect. Our attitude toward His name should be based upon the words expressed so beautifully for us by the apostle Paul: "Therefore God also has highly exalted Him and given Him the name which is above every other name, that at the name of Jesus every knee should bow, of those in heaven, and of those on earth, and of those under the earth, and that every tongue should confess that Jesus Christ is Lord, to the glory of God the Father" (Phil. 2: 9–11). All we do in worship should be done "to the glory of God the Father."

Jesus, Name above all names. Let us speak it most carefully, let us sing it most reverently, let us use it most gladly.

> There is a name that means so much to me,
> Of all the names I've heard there'll never be
> Another name in heaven or earth like Jesus;
> No other one is worthy of all praise.
> For in that name is life, and health, and mercy,
> Yes, in that name is love and joy and peace—
> Though some have tried to tell me there are others,
> No other one could ever take His place.
> **HIS NAME IS JESUS.**[1]

The Significance of the Sabbath

---◆---

That the church needs to become like the world in order to win the world is being promoted by many evangelicals today. We must be careful that we are not more concerned with what the world thinks than with what God thinks.

DEAR CHURCH,

I wonder how many people in the church today really consider the Sabbath to be a holy day, a day set aside for the Lord. God was quite explicit in His fourth commandment to His people: *"Remember the Sabbath day, to keep it holy"* (Exod. 20:8).

Have you ever wondered what was so special about the Sabbath? Many times in Scripture we see God bringing judgment upon His people because they were failing to observe the Sabbath as He had commanded them. Obviously the Sabbath is quite significant to the Lord. If we look at some of God's commands to His people regarding this day, we will see why its observance was so important. In Exodus 31, we hear God saying to Moses, "Speak also to the children of Israel, saying: 'Surely My Sabbaths you shall keep, for it is a sign between Me and you throughout your generations, that you may know that I am the LORD who sanctifies you. You shall keep the Sabbath, therefore, for it is holy to you.' . . . Therefore the children of Israel shall keep the Sabbath, to observe the Sabbath throughout their generations as a perpetual covenant. It is a sign between Me and the children of Israel forever" (vv. 13–14, 16–17).

The Sabbath was given to the children of Israel as a sign of God's covenant with them. They were His people. By observing the Sabbath, the

Israelites testified to the nations around them that they were God's redeemed people, that He and He alone was their God. This distinction set them apart from the ungodly people among whom they lived. The routine of their lives was different. That difference was a testimony to their covenant relationship with God.

This is why the Sabbath was so important to God. By its observance, His people would be reminded that they were His people. They would be reminded of His work in creation, for Scripture records that after six days of creative activity He rested or ceased His work. They would be reminded that He alone was the God they served and worshiped.

Although most Christians no longer observe the seventh day of the week, as the Israelites did, the principle still remains. In the early church, Christians began meeting on the first day of the week in celebration of the resurrection of their Lord, Jesus Christ. This became their special day set aside to meet together in corporate worship and to cease from normal activities. Sunday became known as "the Lord's Day."

Interestingly, it was not just Christians who looked at Sunday in this way. The "world" did as well. Businesses were closed, period. It was the law. Even restaurants, for the most part, were shut because this was the one day the proprietors took off for change and rest. The Sabbath influence was felt everywhere.

The memories I have as a lad growing up in eastern Canada and Switzerland of our attitude toward Sunday stand out in sharp contrast to a lot of the thinking of our day. For starters, Sunday was the Lord's Day. It was the day set apart for corporate worship. We all put on our best clothes, combed our hair a bit more carefully, and went to church. We took extra care because we were going to worship God. We were doing something special. When we entered the meeting hall or sanctuary, there was no running around or talking, for people were praying or reading the Bible. We prepared for the time when we would all worship God together. There was a reverence toward God and toward worship that seems so foreign in many of our churches now.

This attitude toward the Lord's Day followed us out of church into the activities of the day. It was different from all the other days of the week. There were things that we could do all week that we didn't do on Sunday. We sometimes took a walk in the mountains in the afternoon, or we read, or the "old folk" took a nap. It was a day to relax. It was the Lord's Day.

Little by little, however, the attitude toward "the Lord's Day" changed. The laws were rewritten and now, with few exceptions, Sunday is treated just like every other day in the week. Sadly, this is not only true of those in the world; it is true of Christians as well. Why has this happened? One of the obvious reasons has to do with economics. Sunday has become another day to "make a living," another day to earn money. But the deeper, more basic issue is a change in the attitude toward God.

The truth of the matter is, no longer does our nation acknowledge God. He has been rejected in our schools, our government, and every area of public life. It is no wonder that the sign of His covenant, the keeping of His Sabbath as a reminder that He is God, has been rejected as well. The tragedy is that Christians have followed the way of the world.

Let me raise a few "what ifs" that could have made a difference and, I will dare suggest, could still do so if they were taken seriously by believers. What if, when the world changed the law, Christians had not changed but continued to observe the Lord's Day as they always had? What if they had refused to work on Sunday or do any shopping? What if they had simply lived by the convictions they held prior to the change?

History records that when the changes began most of the American church, after briefly protesting, joined the ranks of the world, revealing that convictions regarding the Lord's Day were superficial in the first place. Whether we really believe something is evidenced when we are faced with opposition or persecution. It is then that we demonstrate whether our lives are ruled by conviction or convenience. Once again the church failed to give a living, practical testimony to the world that it lives by a different set of rules and that it serves a different Master.

Olympian Eric Liddell is one whose convictions did not fail, even though he was forced to deny himself that for which he had worked and sacrificed so diligently. The Christian world applauded as they watched him take his stand in the film *Chariots of Fire*. They applauded all the way to the movie theater exit, then rejoined the world that would continue pressing them into its mold.

A recent conversation I had with a pastor vividly illustrates the problem we are facing. In this instance, the issue revolved around the involvement of children in sports. In past years, games had not been scheduled on Wednesday evenings because of midweek church services. That changed, however, and Christian families who had children involved in league sports were asked to adjust accordingly. They didn't have to worry about Sunday, however, because that was still off limits.

Then games began to be scheduled for Sunday afternoons but never starting before 1 P.M. That way Christian families could still make it to church before their games. Families adapted accordingly and during the season rushed from church to playing field.

Inevitably, the time came when games were scheduled on Sunday mornings, and the pastor lamented the fact that "some of our people are having to miss Sunday School and church because of the games." In effect, he was saying that "sports are more important in the life of some of my members than God is." He went on to say that he felt the problem was going to be resolved, since a number of churches in his association were talking about forming a church league so their people would be able to have their sports and be at church as well.

As I thought about that conversation later, I became increasingly disturbed over what I had heard. You see, this was not taking place in some state where there were few churches and the Christian influence would at best be marginal. This was at the heart of the Bible belt. Most of that county's citizens would claim to be Christian, and the majority of those would have their names on a Baptist church membership role. But here, the world of sports was pressing the church into its mold and in essence was saying to the Christians, "If you're going to play ball, forget the Lord's Day as being anything special."

What should the church do? What should Christian parents do? Whether churches should or should not form separate sports leagues is not the issue. The issue is whether Christians, when faced with such choices, are going to allow the world to press them into its mold. *The real issue is worship.*

What if all the Christian parents involved in this particular sports league had given testimony to their convictions by refusing to compromise? In all probability, the league would have had to back down from its decision to play ball on Sunday. What if the pastors of these churches had addressed the real issue and challenged parents and children to bear witness of the faith by choosing to honor the Lord's Day over sports? When was the last time you heard a sermon like that preached?

For the Christian, keeping the Lord's Day should not be a matter of legalism but of respect for what God has said. As the world shows increasingly less respect for the things of God, the contrast between the world and God's people should become increasingly sharper. The church's assignment and the Christian's commission is to shed light in the darkness, not to embrace it and become like it.

I write to you, fellow believers, to remind you that the difference in the way we observe the Lord's Day should be a testimony of our faith to unbelievers, a sign of our covenant relationship with God through Jesus Christ. How we keep that covenant will reveal what is really important to us. It will show what or Whom we truly worship.

Worship
as a Lifestyle

Worship is the response of an adoring heart to the magnificence of God. In the highest sense of the word, it is the occupation of the created with the Creator Himself. It is the pure joy of magnifying the One whose name is above every other name.

DEAR CHURCH,

What a tragedy it is when a believer sees worship only as something that takes place at church on Sunday morning. Yet that is how many think of worshiping God. I write this letter to remind you that worship is so much more. Essentially, it is an attitude of heart that finds expression in the daily living of life. In reality, worship is a *lifestyle*.

When we look at Scripture, we see the truth of this understanding of worship exemplified in many ways. We find the most unlikely situations being turned into worship encounters. Even when, from a human perspective, circumstances would evoke an entirely different response, we often see God's children worshiping.

King David's life is a good example of this. Do you remember when the prophet Nathan confronted David with his sin of murder and adultery? He told him that as a consequence of his sin, his son would die. For six days David pled for the child's life. Then on the seventh day, the child died. In this encounter with God, David's response demonstrated why he was called "a man after God's own heart." When confronted with his sin, he repented immediately. And rather than responding in anger or rebellion when God did not spare the life of his son, "David arose from the ground, washed and anointed himself, and changed his clothes; and he went into the house of the LORD and worshiped" (2 Sam. 12:20).

David recorded his attitude of heart and lifestyle of worship in Psalm 51, where we find him crying out to God: "Against You, You only, have I sinned, And done this evil in Your sight" (v. 4). He continued by asking the Lord to restore the joy of his salvation, his communion with the Lord. Then he revealed an understanding of God that is so needed in our day: "You do not desire sacrifice, or else I would give it; You do not delight in burnt offering. The sacrifices of God are a broken spirit, A broken and a contrite heart— These, O God, You will not despise" (vv. 16–17).

David's response revealed the heart of a person who understood what God is looking for in true worshipers. His primary concern was for what God thought and what God desired from him, not what he had failed to receive from God. When we have a lifestyle of worship, this will be our response as well. The questions we ask will be, "What does God think? What does He want from me in worship?" instead of "Why is God doing this to me?"

From David's life we see that our responses to God reveal whether we have a worshiping heart. When God calls us to repent, do we respond, or do we rebel? When God is bringing discipline into our lives, do we resist, or do we worship?

I remember the first time I noticed the significant part worship played in Joshua's life. Look at the encounter that Joshua had with the angel of the Lord in Joshua 5:13–14: "And it came to pass, when Joshua was by Jericho, that he lifted his eyes and looked, and behold, a Man stood opposite him with His sword drawn in His hand. And Joshua went to Him and said to Him, 'Are You for us or for our adversaries?' So He said, 'No, but as Commander of the army of the LORD I have now come.' And Joshua fell on his face to the earth and *worshiped,* and said to Him, 'What does my LORD say to His servant?'"

Can you believe it? Joshua was in the process of figuring out how he was going to capture the city of Jericho, and in a moment's time he moved from military strategy to worship. Joshua met the Lord in the course of the living of that day. He didn't plan it, but he was ready for it because his heart was inclined to worship.

Worship is not something you reserve for certain times. It's not just for your quiet time or when you attend a worship service. Worship is a lifestyle. I am writing to remind you that we were created to worship God. *We are worshipers,* and the inward response of worshiping hearts to any encounter with our Lord, no matter where we may find ourselves, is to fall on our faces and worship.

All of us need to ask ourselves whether we have that kind of heart. Are there times in our daily living when we just have to stop and worship; or is worship, in our minds, strictly reserved for our quiet time or church?

Job is another one who had a worshiper's heart. When he learned of the loss of his animals, his servants, and his children, Job's response was to worship! "Then Job arose, tore his robe, and shaved his head; and he fell to the ground and *worshiped.* And he said: 'Naked I came from my mother's womb, And naked shall I return there. The LORD gave, and the LORD has taken away; Blessed be the name of the LORD" (Job 1:20–21, italics added).

At the moment of life's deepest despair, we find Job falling to the ground and worshiping God. Here is an example of one who did not cease to be what he had been created to be, even when faced with his greatest tragedy.

To the believers in Thessalonica the apostle Paul gave these instructions: "In everything give thanks; for this is the will of God in Christ Jesus for you" (1 Thess. 5:18). This verse has not been put in Scripture to mock us but to encourage us. When we are able to maintain God's perspective in the middle of disaster or intense pain, the Holy Spirit can begin work as our Comforter. Job was sustained through all the difficulty he faced because he never ceased to be a worshiper. The most significant worship rising to God's ears may very well come from a valley of death or through a fountain of tears. It rises to Him when, by faith, one of His children looks up and says, "Lord, I don't understand, and it doesn't make human sense, but I praise You. . . . I worship You. . . . I thank You." *From the midst of great crisis may rise our deepest worship.*

Several years ago the Lord graciously brought me to a deeper understanding of this. I was on one of my early-morning runs. It was at a time when we found ourselves weighted down with serious financial and personnel problems at the International Christian Center in Switzerland. It all seemed quite insurmountable, humanly speaking at least, and I was in one of those "human" periods. As I ran, the problems kept recycling in my mind.

Suddenly I looked up into the night sky. At that very moment, one of the brightest, closest shooting stars I had ever seen crossed the sky above me. It was followed by another. I immediately forgot what I had been thinking about as I felt myself drawn heavenward. Perhaps I felt a little bit like David did that night when he marveled at God's handiwork. I stopped and just stared at the stars.

I began to sing and shout at the top of my lungs. No one could hear me on that country road except the cows and, of course, God. He seemed so close. I sensed a need to kneel. It wasn't right to stand any more. I knelt in the middle of the road, wept, and worshiped. I don't know how long I was there, but when I got up and began running again, everything had changed. The problems weren't problems any more. I now saw them as opportunities for God to show Himself as the Provider. It was then that the words to this song were birthed. I started singing:

> When you find that the valley is lonely and deep
> Or the trails of the mountain keep getting more steep;
> In those nights when it's harder to laugh than to weep,
> Have you thought about worshiping God?
> When the sand castles built in the dreams you have dreamed
> Start to crumble and fall, and all hope seems to end;
> When you wish you could turn and start over again,
> Why not stop and try worshiping God.[1]

The words came as naturally as breathing that morning. They came easily . . . when I worshiped.

Fellow worshiper, do you worship, thank, and praise God in the midst of testing, of misunderstanding, and of pain? Or are you more inclined to worship only when life is going well? Do you see God as the One who is to be worshiped, not *even* when things are difficult, but *especially* when they are?

Dr. Vance Havner once said that the reason so few Christians are optimistic is that they have a "misty optic." Is your optic misty, or can you see beyond your problem to the One who is seated on the throne? Until you do, you will not be able to bow and truly worship.

As I bring this letter to a close, I want to remind you of some of the things we have been looking at. First, it would seem that there is no inappropriate time to worship. With Joshua, it happened when he was anticipating battle. With David, it was following God's denial of his request to spare the life of his son. With Job, it was in the midst of life's greatest crisis.

Secondly, worship is a response to who God is. With Joshua, it was when the visitor revealed Himself as Commander of the Lord's army. When David was confronted with God's holiness, he responded in worship. Job worshiped when he recognized God's sovereignty. It is God's prerogative to do what He will. There was no question in Job's mind that God was in charge.

Thirdly, no matter what the circumstances may be, the heart attitude of a worshiper is always the same. Though Joshua's thoughts were on the conquering of Jericho, his heart was ready to worship. Though David was experiencing the consequences of his sin, he worshiped. Though Job faced catastrophe, his first inclination was to bow before his Maker in worship.

And finally, worship is not complete without repentance and surrender. In his response, Joshua showed he was ready to do anything his Commander said: "And Joshua fell on his face to the earth and worshiped, and said to Him, 'What does my Lord say to His servant?'" (Josh. 5:14b). Worshipers are under orders. David's immediate response to God's accusation through Nathan was to repent. The more Job understood who God was, the humbler he became: "I have heard of You by the hearing of the ear, But now my eye sees You. Therefore I abhor myself, and repent in dust and ashes" (Job 42:5–6).

My prayer for all of us is that we will be worshipers, not only at church, but in the nitty-gritty of daily living, for how we respond to what comes to us each day most clearly reveals whether we are worshipers at heart.

Born to Worship

───────◆───────

At creation God placed into man the need to worship.
At "new birth," this need finds its ultimate fulfillment
when man becomes not only a "new creation"
but a "new worshiper" of his Creator.

DEAR CHURCH,

To this point my letters to you have focused on worship in the Old Testament under the Old Covenant. Now I am anxious to share with you some thoughts about worship under the New Covenant.

As the New Testament canon opens, the scene changes. The Promised One has come. Light has entered the world. The One in whom all the fullness of the Godhead dwells has been fleshed out among us. Will this affect how we worship? Will the way we worship change in light of all the prophecies which are being fulfilled? Are we still expected to bow, to prostrate ourselves, to stoop in worship before our God? After all, isn't this the age of celebration?

It doesn't take long to discover that nothing has changed. What worship meant in the past, as taught in Old Testament days, worship still means in the present. The first reference to worship in the New Testament is recorded in Matthew 2:2, where the Magi sought the place where the "King of the Jews" had been born. Their purpose in searching for Him was to worship Him. The word used here is the Greek *proskuneo*, meaning to prostrate oneself in homage, to crouch, to kiss the hand, to reverence and adore the one being worshiped. This word, used predominantly in the New Testament, projects the same image found in the Old Testament word *shachah*. It is the same word

Satan used when, two chapters later in Matthew 4, he tempted the Son of God, saying: "All these things I will give You if You will fall down and *worship* me" (v. 9, emphasis mine).

In my first letter to you, I pointed out that the issue of worship is at the heart of the battle between God and Satan. Before whom will the soul of man bow? Satan knew that if the Son of God could be persuaded to worship him the conflict would be over. The victory would be his. But Jesus' reply settled the matter: "Away with you, Satan! For it is written, 'You shall worship the LORD your God, and Him only you shall serve'" (v. 10).

Our Lord used this same word for worship in His answer to the Samaritan woman's inquiry about the place where worship should take place: "The hour is coming, and now is, when the true worshipers will worship the Father in spirit and truth; for the Father is seeking such to worship Him. God is Spirit, and those who worship Him must worship in spirit and truth" (John 4:23–24). The place for worship has changed. Now it is wherever God's people are. But the heart attitude of worship remains the same: to prostrate oneself, to revere, to do homage, to adore.

Once again we see the picture—if not physically, then attitudinally—of bowing before God. The issue under the New Covenant is the same as under the old: Worship centers on the attitude of the heart. The questions we must ask ourselves remain the same: Are we willing to bow to the will, confess the pride, and surrender the life?

It does not take much more than a glance at the New Testament to realize that the heartbeat of worship under the New Covenant is Jesus Christ. The early church's worship was shaped by their understanding of who God was and what He did in Christ. The worship of New Covenant believers was and always will be through Christ, in Christ, and for Christ. It is a response to the nature of God and His Self-revelation through His Son. I don't think we can state this too strongly. New Testament worship is a response to who God is in Christ.

Hebrews 11:6b tells us, "He who comes to God must believe that He is. . . ." That He is what? That He is who He says He is in Scripture. If we are to worship God acceptably, we must believe that He is who He says He is. But why is it that, with His unquestionably clear revelation of Himself, so much more time and effort is concentrated today on analyzing ourselves, the creature, than seeking to understand Him, the Creator? A cursory glance at the shelves of our Christian bookstores reveals that much more is being written today about getting to know ourselves than getting to know God.

True worship is fundamentally objective, not subjective. The object and audience of our worship is God. It begins with Him, and it must end with Him. And everything in between is of Him and for Him. In fact, the restoration of relationship with Him at our new birth begins with worship. We were created to worship Him!

I want to show you an example in the Gospels that is not usually thought of as addressing the matter of worship. I believe, however, that this paraphrased account of the healing of a blind man in John 9:1–38 and of his subsequent conversion may be one of the most powerful examples of not only what worship is but also its significance in our coming to faith. Through it we may come to understand more clearly that worship is not something "out there" that we do; it is something "in here" that we are.

Picture with me a day in the life of this one who had been born to bring glory to God. He had awakened that morning, expecting that day to be no different than all the others had been since he had started begging on the streets of Jerusalem. He had never seen the light of day. From birth he had depended on his hearing and touch. These senses had increased in sensitivity over the years, so his hearing could easily pick up the conversations of passersby, even as he begged for alms.

This day, however, would prove to be amazingly different from any other he had experienced. It began with a conversation he overheard from an approaching group. As they neared the place where he was sitting, he realized *he* was the subject of their conversation: "Rabbi, was this man born blind because he sinned, or because of the sin of his parents?"

"Neither," someone answered. "He was born blind so that the works of God might be revealed in him. I must do the work of the one who sent me while it is day." It grew quiet for a few moments. Then suddenly, the strangest thing happened. Someone was putting something on his eyes! And the one who did it told him to go and wash it off in the pool of Siloam, (John 9:3–4, paraphrased).

As strange as this seemed, he decided he had nothing to lose. Aided by the crowd that had gathered, he went and washed in the pool. At this point, the unbelievable happened. What he had occasionally dreamed of, but never had been able to really hope for, became a reality. He could see! He actually could see. He didn't need his cane any more. He didn't need friends to help him make his way. Now he could see.

His excitement drew an even larger crowd, and those who recognized him as the blind beggar were astonished. How could this be? They began quizzing him, asking how it had happened and who had healed him. When he told them, they wanted to know where Jesus was now. Though he had been told that it was Jesus who had healed him, he had no idea where He had gone.

The crowd decided to take him to the synagogue. Perhaps they were curious to see what the Pharisees would say, since this had taken place on the Sabbath. The Pharisees asked the same questions the crowd had asked. They immediately determined that the one who had done the healing could not be from God since he had done it on the Sabbath. The crowd was divided over this. Some asked how a sinner could do anything so miraculous. The Pharisees then asked the healed blind man what he thought of Jesus. He told them that he thought He must be a prophet.

Finally the religious leaders sent for his parents. His parents confirmed that he was indeed their son and that he had been born blind. When asked how it was that he could now see, they said that the Pharisees needed to ask their son, since he was of age. Actually, they were afraid of saying too much, for they were members of the synagogue. Word had already been spread that anyone who believed Jesus was the Christ would be excommunicated.

The religious leaders began the interrogation again. They tried to get the man to say something negative about Jesus, but he wouldn't. He only marveled that they thought Jesus was a sinner while being faced with the proof of His having healed a man born blind. He finally said something that turned out to be more than the religious leaders could handle; he asked them whether they were wanting to become Jesus' disciples too, since they were showing so much interest in what He had done. For this, they threw him out of the synagogue.

As he walked away from the synagogue with perfect sight, most of us would probably agree that nothing could really surpass what had already happened to him that day. Yet the most significant event was still to come. He had been healed. He had done the best he could to witness to what had happened. He had even called Jesus a prophet. There had been a lot of excitement. An awareness of the power of God had been awakened in his spirit. Now he certainly was more interested in spiritual things than before. At this point, he probably could have joined his parents in attending the synagogue on a regular basis, and for the rest of his life he would have been ready to tell of the time and place it had all happened. So what else, you say, could there be? What more do you want?

This brings us to the main point. It isn't that the blind man has been physically healed, but it is what we see happening in the Father's process of drawing that man to His Son. In spite of the healing, in spite of all the excitement, in spite of his confessing that he thought Jesus was a prophet, this man was still lost. This account is not so much about physical healing as it is about *spiritual conversion.* After all, what good is physical healing and a lot of excitement if nothing of eternal value takes place?

Notice what happens next in the story: "Jesus heard that they had cast him out; and when He had found him, He said to him, 'Do you believe in the Son of God?' He answered and said, 'Who is He, Lord, that I may believe in Him?' And Jesus said to him, 'You have both seen Him and it is He who is talking with you.' Then he said, 'Lord, I believe!' And he worshiped Him" (John 9:35–38).

Do you see the significance of what is happening? The Lord Jesus has sought this man out and revealed Himself as the Messiah, the Son of God. The healed blind man in whom God has been working responds immediately with a resounding, "'Lord, I believe!' And he worshiped Him." He prostrated himself and bowed before the One he now recognized as Lord.

There are at least four things I want you to observe in this divine encounter, and I believe each of these relates to us today. First, *though the man was physically healed, he was not yet a believer.* His response to Jesus makes this clear: "Who is He, Lord, that I might believe in Him?" (v. 36). From this we see that one can experience a miracle of healing from God and still be lost.

Secondly, *there is no salvation without revelation.* "You have both seen Him and it is He who is talking with you" (v. 37). Although the man could be physically healed, he could not believe until Jesus revealed Himself as Savior. Belief is a response to God's work of grace in revealing Himself to us. The man knew that his greatest need was spiritual, and he recognized that the answer to his need was standing before him. His response was evidence of the Father's drawing of the man to His Son.

Thirdly, *there is no redemption without an attitude of worship.* "'Lord, I

believe!' And he worshiped Him" (v. 38). The moment this man realized that
Jesus was the Messiah, he responded with the response of a humble, worshiping
heart. Anyone who speaks the words "Lord, I believe," but in his heart will
not stoop to worship the Savior has not experienced God's saving grace.

I believe this story has more to teach us about salvation than we may realize.
There are people today who, because they have had some kind of experience
or have shown an interest in spiritual things or have just started to ask
questions, are prematurely baptized into the membership of our churches. If
this healed blind man had walked down a church aisle today, more often than
not he would have been welcomed, baptized into the fellowship, and encouraged
to share his testimony within hours. He had said the right words. He had
been healed by the Lord . . . but he was still lost. A tragedy? Yes, for the real
issue is not what experiences a person has had or whether he shows signs of
interest in the things of God, but rather, is there evidence of new birth?

An awakened interest in spiritual things is often simply that—an interest.
Though that may be all there is, we often interpret this interest as faith, and
before you know it an unconverted person is "in the fold." We then dutifully
instruct him in how to "live the Christian life"—attend church, join a Sunday
School class, attend Bible study—when, in fact, he hasn't yet met the Savior.
Then we wonder why the person does not show any desire for God's Word,
prayer, tithing, service through the church, or regularly attending worship
meetings.

What is the problem? These have no capacity to worship God, for they
have never bowed before the Savior in repentance. *The soul who has never
bowed to worship knows no redemption.* I wonder how many members in our
churches today have said the words "I believe" but have never bowed to worship.
But it is also true that *the soul who has once bowed but no longer worships is
living in disobedience.*

In Isaiah 57:15, we read: "For thus says the High and Lofty One Who
inhabits eternity, whose name is Holy: 'I dwell in the high and holy place,
With him who has a contrite and humble spirit.'" I don't know of a better way
to put it than to call what takes place at conversion "repentant worship."
Since, as we just read in Isaiah, it is among this kind of people God dwells,
doesn't it stand to reason that this same attitude of *repentant worship* would be
the womb for new birth? Anyone "making a profession" with any other attitude
does not understand what salvation is. They don't understand their

lostness and the grace that is offered to them. This former blind man did. It was therefore not coincidental that when Jesus revealed Himself to him, he *worshiped*, for the very meaning of worship is to bow and to humble oneself. What other response could there be to God's mercy?

Finally, just as there is no salvation without repentance—"Repent therefore and be converted, that your sins may be blotted out" (Acts 3:19)—there is no true repentance without humbling ourselves before God. In the very act of repenting you find the heart attitude of worship. Our eternal life with God begins at new birth with a worshiping heart. It was for this purpose that we were created. This life of worship then continues for the rest of our lives here on earth, as we grow in grace.

But that is not the end, for as we see in the last book of the Bible, the Book of the Revelation, worship will continue throughout all eternity. *Worship is forever! It was for this that we were born again. It is to be the essence of our living, for out of worship issues everything else in life.*

Dear church member, do you have a worshiping heart? Are you a worshiper?

LETTER 10

Worship and the Glory of God

*Worship is the adoring response of the creature to the infinite majesty of God.
While it presupposes submission to Him, to worship, in the highest sense,
is not supplication for needs, or even thanksgiving for blessings,
but the occupation of the soul with God Himself. . . .
The end of it all is the pure joy of magnifying the One who alone is worthy.
—Robert E. Coleman*

DEAR CHURCH,

I have written to you before about the significant role worship played in
the activity of heaven in eternity past. We saw that the issue of worship was at
the heart of Lucifer's rebellion against God as he tried to rally the hosts of
heaven to bow down to him. Beginning with this letter, I want to look through
the eyes of the apostle John as God opened a door into heaven and showed
him things that "must shortly take place" (Rev. 1:1). Then I want to apply
what we see to the worship in our own personal lives and in our churches.

I think it is especially interesting and significant to note that the revelation of our Lord to John on the Isle of Patmos began with very personal letters
to seven churches. Before John was allowed to observe what was taking place
in heaven, the Lord would address what was taking place on earth. And what
was taking place on earth was not very encouraging.

To five of the seven churches, our Lord issued a severe warning. You
might even say He gave them an ultimatum. After commending several of
them for the good things in which they were involved, to all five he said,
"Repent or else!" Think about the significance of this warning. This was the
early church. This was the church that had earned the reputation of turning

the world upside down. This was the church that had experienced such phenomenal growth. This was the church that was willing to lay down its life for
the Lord, and many in the church had done just that. Now, even before the
last apostle had died, this church was showing the same propensity to back-
slide and turn away from God as His people had shown so many times before
in past generations. The influence of the world had crept in and was beginning to shape the church. Does this sound familiar?

In His message to the church at Ephesus, Jesus exposed the hearts of the
people and showed how they had left their first love. He admonished them to
look back and see how far they had fallen. Then He warned them of the consequences of not repenting and turning back to Him. His message was clear:
"Repent or else!"

His warnings to the churches of Pergamum and Thyatira concerned the
matters of eating food which had been offered in worship to idols and of sex-
ual sin. Again came the warning: "Repent or else!" The church in Sardis was
the one church everyone thought was alive and thriving, yet Jesus accused
them of being dead. He warned them to wake up and repent, or He would
come as a thief in the night.

To the church in Laodicea that considered itself to be rich He said, "You are
wretched, miserable, poor, blind, and naked" (Rev. 3:17). He rebuked them for
being lukewarm and admonished them to repent. He then portrayed Himself in
a picture that may very well describe a good portion of the North American
church today: He stands on the outside of the church door knocking. While the
church goes on with its activities, *while the church worships*, it is completely
unaware that the Lord has been shut out and is on the outside *waiting* for someone to open the door. In essence, the Lord Jesus was restating one of the last
messages delivered to God's people through the prophets almost five hundred
years before: "Return to Me, and I will return to you" (Zech. 1:3; Mal. 3:7).

Then, after rebuking the churches on earth that were offering Him unacceptable worship, our Lord opened a door to heaven and invited the beloved,
exiled apostle John to observe what no human eyes had ever seen: *the perfect
worship of heaven itself!* "Come up here," the Lord said. John provided us with a
detailed account of what he saw.

> After these things I looked, and behold, a door standing open in
> heaven. And the first voice which I heard was like a trumpet

speaking with me, saying, "Come up here, and I will show you things which must take place after this." Immediately I was in the Spirit; and behold, a throne set in heaven, and One sat on the throne. And He who sat there was like a jasper and a sardius stone in appearance; and there was a rainbow around the throne, in appearance like an emerald. Around the throne were twenty-four thrones, and on the thrones I saw twenty-four elders sitting, clothed in white robes; and they had crowns of gold on their heads. And from the throne proceeded lightnings, thunderings and voices. Seven lamps of fire were burning before the throne, which are the seven Spirits of God. Before the throne there was a sea of glass, like crystal. And in the midst of the throne, and around the throne, were four living creatures full of eyes in front and in back. The first living creature was like a lion, the second living creature like a calf, the third living creature had a face like a man, and the fourth living creature was like a flying eagle. The four living creatures, each having six wings, were full of eyes around and within. And they do not rest day or night, saying: "Holy, holy, holy, Lord God Almighty, Who was and is and is to come!" Whenever the living creatures give glory and honor and thanks to Him who sits on the throne, who lives forever and ever, the twenty-four elders fall down before Him who sits on the throne and worship Him who lives forever and ever, and cast their crowns before the throne, saying: "You are worthy, O Lord, To receive glory and honor and power; For You created all things, And by Your will they exist and were created" (Rev. 4:1–11).

A picture of the worship of heaven! This is the perfect worship that pleases the heart of God. What better place to turn to help us understand the true nature of worship.

The first thing John wrote about in this chapter was a throne. "And behold, a throne set in heaven, and One sat on the throne." This throne seemed to be the dominant image in John's mind, for he mentioned it ten times in this one chapter. The focal point of heaven's worship is the One seated on the throne.

Perhaps it would help if we had a better understanding of the significance of a throne. A throne portrays sovereignty and authority. In this case, the throne portrays One who has absolute authority and complete sovereignty. It is the throne of the Lord God Almighty.

When we come to worship, we come to a throne. This is where worship must begin. Everything else arranges itself around that throne. All created life, the church, the angelic world—*everything* is in subjection to the One seated on the throne. When we worship, we acknowledge that all authority, power, dominion, control, and supremacy belong to Him who sits on the throne. There is no authentic worship without the acknowledgment of the authority of God.

The prophet Isaiah came face to face with this same throne: "In the year that King Uzziah died, I saw the Lord sitting on a throne, high and lifted up" (Isa. 6:1). News of King Uzziah's death had reached his ears, and in grief he made his way to the temple to seek God. It may very well have been that the earthly throne of Uzziah had clouded Isaiah's vision up to that point in his life. Not only was he the king's scribe; but according to the Talmud, he was also King Uzziah's cousin. In any case, the king's death caused Isaiah to do some reevaluating, and he knew where he needed to turn; he turned to the Lord.

Before Isaiah could see God, he had to lose sight of the earthly throne. You might say he had to lose sight to truly see. Maybe this doesn't make sense from the world's perspective, but in God's economy things are often just the opposite of what the world says. With God, in order to see, you have to lose sight. With God, to find you must lose. With God, to live you must die.

In the busyness of our living, we often don't slow down long enough to seek God and give Him time to speak to us. Nor do we stand in wonder and reverence of our awesome God, because our vision may be clouded by other thrones.

When the church gathers to worship on any given Sunday morning, what do they see? Is it really God they see high and lifted up, or are there a multitude of other things standing in the way of their meeting Him? Where is the focus of attention? Are these gathered Christians ever brought to a point of bowing, of falling on their faces—if not literally, then in the attitude of their hearts—before the Lord as Isaiah did when he encountered the throne in his vision?

Ezekiel was another prophet who had a vision of this same throne. In his description of the One seated on the throne, he said, "This was the appearance of the likeness of the glory of the Lord. So when I saw it, I fell on my face" (Ezek. 1:28).

How does the picture of what John saw of worship in heaven compare with what we do in our churches? The church today preaches, evangelizes, organizes, celebrates, fellowships, and has "a good time," but how often does the church really worship?

It seems that in the context of worship today, many times it is not God seated on His throne that people see. Instead they see an exhibition of human ability. They hear music, but do they hear God? They hear preaching, but do they meet God? They may enjoy a good performance, but do they have an encounter with Almighty God?

Often people perform on the platforms of our churches, and rather than the congregation of worshipers seeing the glory of God and seeing themselves in light of that glory, they are seeing a person in all his glory. Today, especially in the realm of church music, *God is often being used to display man's talent rather than man's talent being used to display God.*

God has made clear that He will not share His glory with anyone. "I am the LORD, that is My name; and My glory I will not give to another" (Isa. 42:8). We cannot claim for ourselves the glory that belongs to God alone and expect our worship to be acceptable to Him. When we worship, we need to see God, not the talents of people. I believe this is one of the areas of our worship that deeply grieves the heart of God. Perhaps the words of this song express it best:

> Have you been called to serve where others tried and failed,
> And with God's help and strength your efforts have prevailed?
> Touch not the glory!
>
> Have you some special gift, some riches you can share,
> Or are you called of God to intercessory prayer?
> Touch not the glory!
>
> Has God appointed you to some great noble cause,
> Or put you where you hear the sound of man's applause?
> Touch not the glory!
>
> A watching world still waits to see what can be done
> Through one who touches not that which is God's alone.
> Touch not the glory, touch not the glory, touch not the glory
> For it belongs to God![1]

God will not share His throne or His glory with anyone, no matter how wonderful and talented men and women may think they are. The moment we raise ourselves up to take the glory that is God's alone, the manifest presence of God departs from that service. Could that be why He may be on the outside of many of our churches, knocking, while we are inside enjoying ourselves?

Dear church, we must not give to others the glory that belongs to God alone and call it worship. The psalmist said in Psalm 29:1–2: "Give unto the LORD, O you mighty ones, Give unto the LORD glory and strength. Give unto the LORD the glory due to His name; Worship the LORD in the beauty of holiness." When you gather to worship, remember: Don't touch the glory!

It matters not if the world has heard, or approves, or understands; The only applause we're meant to seek is the applause of nail-scarred hands.

Worship and the Authority of God

So speaks our Lord to us: "You call me Master, and you do not obey me.
You call me Light, and you do not see me. You call me The Way, and you do not walk
with me. You call me Life, and you do not live by me. You call me Wise,
and you do not listen to me. You call me Kind, and you do not love me.
You call me Rich, and you do not ask of me. You call me Eternal,
and you do not seek me. If I condemn you, do not blame me."
—from an engraving in the cathedral of Lubeck, Germany

DEAR CHURCH,

There is so much we can learn from the apostle John's observation of the worship of heaven. I believe we could study his revelation for the rest of our lives and never exhaust its riches. Let's look more closely at what John saw and heard: "And every creature which is in heaven and on the earth and under the earth and such as are in the sea, and all that are in them, I heard saying: 'Blessing and honor and glory and power Be to Him who sits on the throne, And to the Lamb, forever and ever!'" (Rev. 5:13).

Notice what was happening here. *Every creature* was proclaiming that all blessing and honor and glory and power belong to God and to the Lamb. And God is sitting on the throne.

As I mentioned in an earlier letter to you, a serious hindrance to true worship is the view of God many people have today. This is really at the heart of the worship problem we are facing. The problem is not styles or musical tastes; the real problem is with how we see God. The way we live on a daily basis reveals our view of God, as does the way we worship.

The God we worship is the One who has absolute authority and complete sovereignty over all things. Nothing ever happens that is beyond His control. In fact, Jesus said that not even a sparrow falls to the ground apart from the Father's will (Matt. 10:29). I believe many believers do not really grasp the import of this reality. Imagine how different things would be if we lived our lives consistently with this view in mind. What a difference it would make in our reactions to life if we were to keep sight of the throne when we faced the unexpected or when tragedy struck. The actions and attitudes of Christians would be radically different from those of unbelievers. Their lives would bear witness of their faith, as it should.

I believe that a fundamental problem with much of our worship today, and with our lives in general, is that we don't see God as the God whose throne is really above the world. We don't see Him as the God who lives outside of time. We don't see Him as Moses saw Him: "Lord, You have been our dwelling place in all generations. Before the mountains were brought forth, Or ever You had formed the earth and the world, Even from everlasting to everlasting, You are God" (Ps. 90:1–2). We don't see Him as He revealed Himself through the prophet Isaiah: "I am God, and there is no other; I am God, and there is none like Me, Declaring the end from the beginning, And from ancient times things that are not yet done" (Isa. 46:9b–10).

It is interesting to contrast the God Moses knew with the gods Israel had begun to worship in Isaiah's day. Instead of remaining true to the One who had delivered them from slavery in Egypt, who had provided for all their needs and led them to rest in the Promised Land, God's people had begun to worship gods that had to be carried on a cart. They had become just like the ungodly nations around them. After all God had done for these people, they had turned to idols of their own making that had to be carried. With a grieved heart, God reminded them of all the times He had borne them; He had carried them from the womb until old age, and not once had they ever had to carry Him (Isa. 46:1–7).

Before we judge the Israelites too harshly, let's look at what the church is doing today. It often seems as though we, like the Israelites, have the idea that we have to carry God, rather than His carrying us. We act as if we think *we* are the ones responsible for building the church, when Jesus said clearly, "I will build My church" (Matt. 16:18).

Have you ever wondered why so many pastors today are becoming weary and are dropping out of the ministry? Why are so many of them discouraged?

I think it is often because their view of God is of one who sits on a cart, a god that has to be pulled. Some pastors see the church as sitting on a cart and believe that if it is going to grow they are going to have to pull it. As they pull, they have to be ever so careful that it doesn't tilt, or half the church will fall off! They see it as their responsibility to keep everybody happy rather than pointing the people to God and teaching them to be holy.

Do we worship a god of wood? Some do. Their god is something they have created, built, or bought. Rather than their life being hidden in and existing in God, it consists of outward man-made creations that have to be carried. The moment something happens to these creations, their world starts falling apart.

I hope you see how this issue relates to our ability to worship God acceptably. How often we worship a lesser God than our God really is. Our God never has and never will need a support system. Our God does not need to be pulled on a cart. He is El Al! He is from everlasting to everlasting. When we gather to worship, this is the God before whom we bow. The psalmist was convinced of this when he wrote: "Happy is he who has the God of Jacob for his help, Whose hope is in the LORD his God, Who made heaven and earth, The sea, and all that is in them; Who keeps truth forever, Who executes justice for the oppressed, Who gives food to the hungry. The LORD gives freedom to the prisoners. . . . The LORD shall reign forever—Your God, O Zion, to all generations. Praise the LORD!" (Ps. 146:5–7, 10).

Worship begins when we acknowledge the authority and sovereignty of God. He sits on a throne! Dear brothers and sisters, let us never forget that when we gather to worship we are approaching a throne, upon which sits the Supreme Sovereign of the universe, the One who has absolute authority over our lives, and in fact, over the universe. Martin Luther gave us a beautiful expression of the authority and sovereignty of God when he wrote:

> A mighty fortress is our God, a bulwark never failing;
> Our helper He, amid the flood of mortal ills prevailing.
> For still our ancient foe doth seek to work us woe—
> His craft and power are great, and, armed with cruel hate,
> On earth is not his equal.
>
> Did we in our own strength confide, our striving would be losing,
> Were not the right Man on our side, the Man of God's own choosing.

You ask who that may be? Christ Jesus, it is He—
Lord Sabaoth, His name, from age to age the same,
And He must win the battle.

And though this world, with devils filled, should threaten to undo us,
We will not fear, for God has willed His truth to triumph through us.
The Prince of Darkness grim, we tremble not for him;
His rage we can endure, for lo, his doom is sure;
One little word shall fell him.

That word above all earthly powers, no thanks to them, abideth;
The Spirit and the gifts are ours through Him who with us sideth.
Let goods and kindred go, this mortal life also;
The body they may kill: God's truth abideth still, His kingdom is
     forever.

May we never forget that the One we approach in worship is One who is from everlasting to everlasting. He has all authority and all power. To Him be all blessing and honor and glory and power.

The Eternity and Activity of God

He is the image of the invisible God, the firstborn over all creation.
For by Him all things were created that are in heaven and that are on earth,
visible and invisible, whether thrones or dominions or principalities or powers.
All things were created through Him and for Him. And He is before all things, and in
Him all things consist. And He is the head of the body, the church, who is the begin-
ning, the firstborn from the dead, that in all things He may have the preeminence.
For it pleased the Father that in Him all the fullness should dwell, and by Him
to reconcile all things to Himself, by Him, whether things on earth or things in
heaven, having made peace through the blood of His cross.
—Colossians 1:15–20

DEAR CHURCH,

In my last two letters to you we have been looking at worship in heaven through the eyes of the apostle John. We have seen that John's mind seemed dominated by the throne he saw and the perpetual worship of heaven.

Dear fellow worshipers, I am writing to remind you that when we come to worship, we too are coming to a throne. Not only do we come to the throne to acknowledge the sovereignty and authority of God; we also acknowledge *the eternity of God.* Notice John's observation: "Whenever the living creatures give glory and honor and thanks to Him who sits on the throne, who lives forever and ever, the twenty-four elders fall down before Him who sits on the throne and worship Him *who lives forever and ever*" (Rev. 4:9–10, italics added). We worship "Him who lives forever and ever." We acknowledge His authority over time and space. He is the One whose very name means "I Am the great I Am." We worship the One for whom a thousand years is as a day—the One who is not bound, as we are, by a watch or a calendar.

In worship we acknowledge that there was a time when we were not, but there never was a time when God was not. God does not exist in time; time exists in God. God does not exist in space; space exists in God. God is eternal in His very essence, which means He is eternal in everything He does. He always acts from an eternal perspective. He never works for time alone. All He does is in accordance with His eternal purposes, which He accomplished in Christ Jesus our Lord.

God's creation of man was not a short-term experiment. He created man for a love relationship that would last for eternity. The moment we are birthed into the family of God, our eternity with Him begins. God had and has an eternal commitment to those who come to Him through His Son, Jesus Christ! God's plans encompass *forever.* Everything God does has eternal consequences. *This is the God we worship!*

"For since the creation of the world His invisible attributes are clearly seen, being understood by the things that were made, even His *eternal power and Godhead,* so that they are without excuse" (Rom. 1:20, italics added). When we worship we acknowledge the foreverness of God; we proclaim the eternity of the One who sits on the throne.

But not only does John see those surrounding the throne affirming the "eternity" of God; he hears them acknowledging *His activity.* "You are worthy, O Lord, to receive glory and honor and power; *for You created all things,* and by Your will they exist and were created" (Rev. 4:11, italics added).

When we worship, we acknowledge God's activity in creation. He created *all things.* This is what John heard the elders saying in heaven. When we worship, we acknowledge that He is the Creator of our human bodies, as fascinating as they are. Each one of us is composed of over ten trillion cells, with each cell containing the complete genetic code, or pattern, for everything that person is. God created a body that is able to pass on all of its genetic material each time a new cell is formed. To form even one cell, an exact copy of at least 100,000 genes must be made, and even one error in replication could result in the death of that cell. Yet every minute, about three billion cells in our bodies die, and are immediately replaced by three billion new cells. What an incredible, awesome God we worship!

When we gather to worship, we are worshiping the One by whose hand the universe was formed. He is the Creator of those stars and galaxies that lie billions of light years from our little planet, that vast space that man continues to reach toward. Yet the farther he goes, the deeper the universe becomes. Astronomers are now telling us that many of those "lights" we see with the naked eye, the ones we think are stars, are really groups of stars called galaxies. They believe that there may be as many as one hundred billion galaxies, each containing as many as one hundred billion stars.

Some time ago I read of a discovery that had just been made using the Hubbell telescope to study one of these galaxies. Astronomers had located what they believe to be the largest black hole in space. It is in Galaxy M87, in the Constellation Virgo. This galaxy is fifty million light years from earth. Light travels at approximately six trillion miles a year, so the distance in miles can be calculated by multiplying fifty million by six trillion. This distance, however, was not as awesome to me as their description of the density of that black hole from which no light can escape. They compared its density to the compacting of planet earth down to the size of a marble that you could hold in your hand. All the continents, all the mountains—all of earth in the palm of your hand!

When I read this, I began to weep. I wept for myself, for I realized I had lost the wonder of the God of creation. I realized that the busyness of life had stolen the awe I once had. I recalled how, as a teenager, I used to climb the mountains around the valley where my family's hotel was located in Switzerland. I remember my favorite spot on the roof of an old abandoned chalet where I would sit and dream and wonder. I realized that I had lost the wonder. It's so easy to lose the wonder, even right in the middle of ministry.

Some friends of ours have given me a very fine telescope. I have had a large skylight cut in the roof of my attic study. When I am home and the night sky is clear, I sometimes open up that skylight and look at those lights my Father created, and I wonder . . . and I worship.

Why is it that the more we learn about God's creation, the less in awe we are of the Creator? The psalmist didn't know a fraction of what we know today about the universe. Yet when he looked into the night skies, from deep within his worshiping heart he cried, "The heavens declare the glory of God; and the firmament shows His handiwork. Day unto day utters speech, and night unto night reveals knowledge" (Ps. 19:1–2). I wonder: Can we worship, if we do not wonder?

The popular hymn "How Great Thou Art" inspires a worshiper to recapture a sense of awe. Have you lost the wonder of the God of creation? Reread the hymn words, or sing it as a prayer to God. When we worship, we worship an awesome God who created all things!

But John observed something more in his vision of heaven. Not only were the elders worshiping the God of Creation; they were worshiping the *God of Redemption.* In the center of the throne, John saw a Lamb: "Then I saw a Lamb, looking as if it had been slain, standing in the center of the throne, encircled by the four living creatures and the elders . . . Then I looked and heard the voice of many angels, numbering thousands upon thousands, and ten thousand times ten thousand. They encircled the throne and the living creatures and the elders. In a loud voice they sang: 'Worthy is the Lamb, who was slain, to receive power and wealth and wisdom and strength and honor and glory and praise!' Then I heard every creature in heaven and on earth and under the earth and on the sea, and all that is in them, singing: 'To him who sits on the throne and to the Lamb be praise and honor and glory and power, for ever and ever!' The four living creatures said, 'Amen,' and the elders fell down and worshiped" (Rev. 5:6a, 11–14 NIV).

In chapter 5 of John's Revelation, we discover that the highest praise, the loudest hallelujahs, the greatest crescendo of worship and adoration are reserved for what God did in redemption. It was a Lamb they were worshiping! John saw "a Lamb looking as if it had been slain." It was the Lamb of God with scars in His hands, His feet, His side, and His brow. It was the Lamb they were falling down before, because the God who flung those one hundred billion galaxies into space is the same God who came to earth, hung on a cross, and died. He died for you! He died for me!

God had made it clear from the very beginning that the only way sin could be cleansed or forgiven was that something, or someone, had to die. I want to trace in Scripture what a dear Presbyterian friend of ours, John L. Fain, calls the "bloodstream of redemption." This stream finds its beginning in the garden of Eden, when animals have to die in order for God to clothe Adam and Eve. This is the first death recorded in Scripture, and it was the result of sin. The next recorded death occurs when we find Abel offering a blood sacrifice to God. The kind of offering God is looking for is made evident when He accepts Abel's sacrifice of a lamb, but rejects Cain's bloodless sacrifice. At that moment God began painting a picture, and with each added color and nuance the message would become clearer: "without shedding of blood there is no remission for sin" (Heb. 9:22). That day, the blood of one lamb was sufficient for the sins of one man.

The picture continues to develop as we follow the stream through the Bible and discover that at the Passover in Egypt, the blood of one lamb becomes sufficient for an entire household, a family. We hear God telling the Israelites that He is going to send one more plague and in that plague He is going to take the life of the firstborn of every family, except for those who would take the blood of a blemishless lamb and sprinkle it over the door to their homes and up and down the sides as well. God said that when He saw the blood He would not touch anyone behind that door. A lamb for a family!

As we continue, the picture becomes increasingly clear in Leviticus as God gives instruction regarding the Day of Atonement, which the children of Israel were now to observe. We hear Him giving intricate, detailed orders to Aaron, the high priest, on exactly what he was to wear and what he was to do. The special day involved offerings for himself, his family, and the releasing of the scapegoat into the wilderness. Finally the day would climax when the high priest entered the holy of holies with the blood of one goat for the sins of the entire nation for a whole year! "This shall be an everlasting statute for you, to make atonement for the children of Israel, for all their sins, once a year" (Lev. 16:34).

Do you see where this is leading? The blood of one lamb for a man when Abel offered his sacrifice. The blood of one lamb for a family at the Passover in Egypt. The blood of one goat for the sins of an entire nation for a whole year on the Day of Atonement. Then, as the final brush stroke of Calvary is added to the canvas, the complete picture is revealed at last—a picture of God's limitless love, a cross where the Lamb is being slain for, not just a man, not just a family, not just a nation, but this Lamb is being slain *for a world* that includes you and me.

There would never be another sacrifice for sin. That day it was paid in full. When Jesus cried *tetelestai* from the cross, He was declaring that it was finished—the picture of the sacrifice was complete. God would require no more blood for sin. The final payment had been made! Sin was paid in full! Hallelujah!

> O Lamb of God, how great Your condescension, ordained before the
>   earth was hung in space
> O Lamb of God, the Author of redemption, You left your glorious
>   throne to take our place.

No other lamb was found in all God's heaven, to satisfy the awesome
  debt of sin,
Except one Lamb, the only Son begotten, *God's just requirements all were
  met in Him!*

At the very outset of our Lord's ministry, it was not coincidental that John
the Baptist declared, "Behold! *The Lamb* of God who takes away the sin of the
world!" (John 1:29, italics added), because standing there before him was the
One who had come to lay down His life for the sins of the world.

Peter said: "Knowing that you were not redeemed with corruptible things,
like silver or gold, from your aimless conduct received by tradition from your
fathers, but with the precious blood of Christ, *as of a lamb* without blemish
and without spot" (1 Pet. 1:18–19, italics added).

John said: "And he (the angel) showed me a pure river of water of life,
clear as crystal, proceeding from the throne of God and *of the Lamb.* . . . And
there shall be no more curse, but the throne of God and *of the Lamb* shall be
in it, and His servants shall serve Him. . . . I, John, saw and heard these
things. And when I heard and saw, I fell down to worship before the feet of
the angel who showed me these things. Then he said to me, 'See that you do
not do that. For I am your fellow servant, and of your brethren the prophets,
and of those who keep the words of this book. *Worship God*'" (Rev. 22:1, 3,
8–9, italics added).

Dear church, when we gather to worship, we need to acknowledge Who
it is we worship. We gather to worship the God of creation! We gather to worship the God of redemption! We gather to worship the Lamb!

The Role of
Submission in Worship

◆

*The apostle John was witness to the highest worship there will ever be as redeemed
humanity removes from its head every sign of achievement and lays it at the feet of
the Lamb. In removing and relinquishing their crowns, they renounce the right to rule
their own lives and turn that right over to Another.*

DEAR CHURCH,

I'm finding that the more I get into this study of worship, the more there
is to be learned. I suppose it really will be a never-ending quest. From what
John saw in the revelation God gave him, there is obviously a lot more to it
than most of us are experiencing today.

Let's look once again at how the apostle John described the worship of
heaven: "Whenever the living creatures give glory and honor and thanks to Him
who sits on the throne, who lives forever and ever, the twenty-four elders fall
down before Him who sits on the throne and worship Him who lives forever
and ever, and *cast their crowns before the throne*" (Rev. 4:9–10, italics added).

There seems to be no question in the hearts of those worshiping as to how
they should respond to the awesome sight of God on the throne. What strikes
me in this scene is that they did not just give glory and honor through words
and song, but they literally "put feet" to their proclamation by *submitting* themselves to the One who sits on the throne. It is one thing to acknowledge the
authority of God and to see Him as the eternal Creator and Redeemer, but it is
quite another thing to respond in a way that shows what we say is what we
really believe. This is not a new concept. It is the same message Jesus gave to
His disciples when He told them that their love for Him would be shown by

their obedience to Him. It is clear that worshiping God through the singing of hymns, choruses, and anthems about His sovereignty, authority, and work in creation and redemption is incomplete if we do not *submit to that authority.*

I confess it is often uncomfortable to place what I think and do against the standard of God's Word. Most of us are quite accustomed to doing things our own way and making excuses for our behavior when it doesn't exactly line up with what we see in Scripture. When the Holy Spirit, our Teacher, convicts us of our hidden sin and calls us to a new depth of repentance and surrender, or opens our eyes to some fresh awareness of truth that requires us to make an adjustment, we are faced with the decision to respond or rebel. I'm ashamed to think of the times I haven't responded well to what God said. It would be easy to get discouraged with my failures, but I take hope in remembering that God is looking for a humble, repentant, teachable heart, and with David I say, "Grant me a willing spirit, to sustain me" (Ps. 51:12 NIV).

God is absolutely uncompromising in His requirements for worship. You see, the way people worship Him reveals where their hearts are. In fact, I believe this is one of the first places where compromise with the world surfaces. Throughout Scripture, God rejected what His people offered Him in worship when their hearts were not in it, even when they were going through the correct form and abiding by the letter of the law. In the final analysis, *worship is and always has been a matter of the heart.*

Why do you suppose John placed so much emphasis on the twenty-four elders "falling down" before Him who sits on the throne? They seem to be doing this over and over. I suppose we don't really need to ask because, if we were honest with ourselves, we'd know that there could be no other appropriate response or reaction to the sovereign, eternal God than to stoop in submission before Him. This brings me to this observation: After watching what is going on in Christian media, looking through the Christian magazines with page after page of glossy promotion of personalities and ministries, and seeing the huge highway billboards promoting pastors, one might wonder if this is not an area where we are sinning rather boldly. It seems that there is a lot more strutting in the American church today than stooping. There is a lot more self-promotion than self-denial. Dear church, this is the antithesis of what the Christian life is supposed to be.

As I think of this issue, I am reminded of what God said to His people back in Isaiah's time: "Thus says the High and Lofty One Who inhabits eternity, whose name is Holy: 'I dwell in the high and holy place, With him who has a contrite and humble spirit, To revive the spirit of the humble, And to revive the heart of the contrite ones'" (Isa. 57:15). I think of how our Lord began His powerful teaching in the Sermon on the Mount: "Blessed are the poor in spirit [humble], For theirs is the kingdom of heaven" (Matt. 5:3). I think of the letter Peter wrote to the churches with these instructions: "All of you be submissive to one another, and be clothed with humility, for 'God resists the proud, But gives grace to the humble'" (1 Pet. 5:5b). Dear friends, do we really think God has changed? From the way many are acting, it would seem as if they do.

It is interesting to note that in what many consider to be God's formula for revival humbling of self precedes everything else: "If My people who are called by My name will humble themselves, and pray" (2 Chron. 7:14). Since this is God speaking, it is significant to note that humbling precedes the offering of prayers that are acceptable to Him. The account of the publican and the Pharisee praying in the Temple clearly reveals the heart attitude God is looking for when His people approach Him. He hears the prayer of the humble heart and receives and glories in the worship and adoration of the contrite and broken spirit.

Many people are talking about and praying for revival today. It is a prominent theme, and many earnestly desire God to grant it to His people. But we must realize that *no revival in history has begun with a self-satisfied people*. All the ones I have read about have started with the humbling and repenting of God's people. Could this be one of the reasons we are not experiencing revival in our day? The motto of the Welsh revival of 1904–05 was "Bend the church and save the world." What a contrast this presents to the self-esteem gospel we hear so much of today! If we are serious in our prayers for revival, we must begin by exhibiting the attitude expressed by the words of this song:

> Bend me lower, lower down at Jesus' feet,
> Holy Spirit, bend me till your work's complete.
> Wash away the stain of sin, make me holy, pure within—
> Bend me lower, lower down at Jesus' feet.

> Bend me lower, lower down at Jesus' feet,
> Holy Spirit, bend me till your work's complete.
> Bend my will and break my pride, surface sins I try to hide,
> Bend me lower, lower down at Jesus' feet.

Bend me lower, lower down at Jesus' feet,
Holy Spirit, bend me till your work's complete.
Flow through me to those around, floods upon the dry parched
     ground—
Bend me lower, lower down at Jesus' feet.[1]

Humbling ourselves in this way is not an easy thing to do. In fact, it probably runs as much counter to our human nature as anything we could do. It strikes at the center of our will. It challenges us in an area that we have been taught to believe is almost as sacred as life itself; it is the matter of "rights."

This is a major issue in the lives of Christians today. It is a major issue in the church. Though God has spoken clearly on this matter and demonstrated it through the life of His Son, we don't seem to want to hear. Perhaps this is why we hear so little preaching on the subject. It certainly is not a popular one in a society that puts so much emphasis on the rights of the individual. In a day when we have gone so far as to give a woman the "right" to take the life of her unborn child, the suggestion that Christians have surrendered their rights is quite distasteful, even unacceptable, to many. Yet the truth must be spoken.

Calling believers to remember that they have abdicated their rights to Christ will not win an election, nor will it get a lot of amens. But it must be faced by Christians today. This is the root cause for the embarrassingly high rate of divorces in the church. It is the root of the shockingly high number of church splits and staff firings. These are symptoms of a serious disorientation to what took place when we were born again.

In his first letter to the church in Corinth, the apostle Paul reminded the believers that they had been bought with a price. I think we sometimes forget what it cost our Lord to purchase our freedom. He gave up His rights to pay the debt of sin by dying on the cross. We are told to have this same mind of Christ operative in us: "Let this mind be in you which was also in Christ Jesus, who, being in the form of God, did not consider it robbery to be equal with God, but made Himself of no reputation, taking the form of a bondservant, and coming in the likeness of men. And being found in appearance as a man, He humbled Himself and became obedient to the point of death, even the death of the cross" (Phil. 2:5–8). We, too, have surrendered our rights for the higher calling of Christ.

I think that the problem with many Christians today is that they have confused the Bill of Rights with a birthright. Even as we cherish the rights we have as citizens of our country, we must be careful to walk humbly before God and before one another, claiming no rights but those of our birthright as children of God, while rejoicing in all the promises included in that birthright, which make us heirs and joint heirs with the One who bought us: Jesus our Savior and Lord.

In his vision of the worship in heaven, the apostle John saw the twenty-four elders not only humbling themselves in submission but also relinquishing, or abdicating, their rights and turning their rights over to another. They demonstrated this by laying their crowns at Jesus' feet. This was a deliberate act on their part as they offered their worship and expressed to Him their allegiance and love.

This is a very moving picture as we see all redeemed humanity, all those who have been washed in the blood of the Lamb, taking from their heads all signs of achievement or accomplishment and laying them at the feet of the Redeemer. It seems obvious that in the removing and relinquishing of their crowns they are renouncing the right to rule their own lives and they are turning that right over to another—*they are relinquishing their rights to the Lamb.* Maybe I could express it best like this:

> My rights? whose rights? God has bought me outright,
> I am no longer my own.
> My rights? whose rights? God has bought me outright
> That through me His glory may be known.
> I belong to God.

Dear church, when you come to worship, remember that you come to a throne. You must come in humility, submitting yourself to the One who is on that throne, to the One you have come to worship.

Service: The Culmination of Worship

———◆———

Anyway, anytime, anywhere, Lord
Serving You every day is my prayer
Take me, Lord, use me, Lord, for Your glory
Anyway, anytime, anywhere.[1]

DEAR CHURCH,

This is the last time I will be writing to you about the worship of heaven as we see it in John's Revelation. In this letter, we are going to see how worship is brought to its completion when the worshiper surrenders in service to the One he worships.

Though the church today places a good bit of emphasis on service, it is not often connected to worship. In reality it should be, because true service *is* worship, and there is no such thing as authentic worship without service. To put it another way, *he who will not serve does not worship.*

True worship is so much more than we generally consider it to be. What God is looking for in worship is not great congregational singing, although that can be honoring to Him. He is not impressed with big choirs and orchestras, though they may bring Him glory. He is not looking for well-articulated prayers or creative preaching, though these may please Him. What God is looking for is *a people who will love Him with all their hearts* and who will demonstrate this love by obeying Him and placing their lives unreservedly in His hands. He is looking for a people who will worship *by serving Him*—not just in church, but every day of their lives.

Jesus said that if we truly love Him, we will show it by keeping His commandments. It is the one who loves Him who offers acceptable sacrifices of praise and worship. Why do we act as though there is no connection between how we live our daily lives and our worship? Do we really think that all there is to worship is good singing and people enjoying themselves? Do we really believe that it doesn't matter to God if we don't plan to serve Him? In today's church it sometimes looks as though the way we *sound* is more important than the way we *serve*. This could not be further from the truth. If I understand Scripture correctly, a congregation of monotones whose hearts are right before the Lord will sound more beautiful to His ears than the four-part harmony of well-trained voices whose offering ceases with their song. What we do speaks louder than what we say or sing. You see:

> God is looking for a people who will crown Him as their Lord;
> Who have turned from earthly idols, all the things this world affords—
> Whose allegiance is unquestioned, caring not what it will cost;
> God is looking for a people who will glory in the cross.

> God is looking for a people who'll *surrender Him their all,*
> With their eyes fixed on the Master, ready at a moment's call
> *To respond to His assignment,* whether short or whether long;
> Willing to change their agenda to the mission God is on.

> God is looking for a people who'll spend time with Him in prayer;
> Those who've died to their ambitions, *who will serve no matter where;*
> Those who seek not earthly treasure, big careers or larger homes—
> God is looking for a people who are His and His alone.[2]

The prophet Isaiah personifies the kind of worshiper God is seeking. At times I have tried, in my imagination, to step inside the temple where Isaiah came face-to-face with our Lord, high and lifted up, sitting on a throne. The death of his cousin, King Uzziah, had caused the earthly throne to lose its meaning, and now Isaiah saw "the" throne. He saw seraphs and heard them calling to one another, "Holy, holy, holy is the LORD of hosts; The whole earth is full of His glory!" (Isa. 6:3). Notice Isaiah's response to what he saw. He was overcome with the awesome presence of God and cried out, "Woe is me, for I am undone! Because I am a man of unclean lips, And I dwell in the midst of a people of unclean lips; for my eyes have seen the King, the LORD of hosts" (v. 5). Immediately after this confession, one of the seraphs touched his lips with a hot coal from the altar, and his sin was cleansed.

It was at this point that one of the most thrilling things of all time happened. Isaiah heard the Trinity speaking: "Whom shall I send, And who will go for Us?" (v. 8). Then, echoing from one corner of the temple to the other, we hear the cry of a worshiping heart. We hear the response of one who has seen the Lord. We hear the words of one whose eyes and ears have been sensitized to the things of God. We hear the words of one who would never be the same again, who would forever be a worshiper of God alone: "Here am I! Send me." (v. 8).

This is the response of one who has worshiped. The apostle Paul made this correlation for those in the church in Rome and for us as well when he said, "I urge you, brothers, in view of God's mercy, to offer your bodies as living sacrifices, holy and pleasing to God—which is your spiritual worship [reasonable service]" (Rom. 12:1 NIV). *True worship culminates in service. He who will not serve is not worshiping God.* The prayer of one who truly worships will be:

> Take these hands, may they serve You in all they do;
> Take this voice, may it speak day and night for You.
> Take these feet, may they walk only in Your ways,
> Take my mind, eyes and ears, use them for Your praise.
> Lord, by Your Spirit use me, may Your light shine through me.
> Lord, with Your life refill me, so the world around will see
> Your hands extended to them, reaching for them,
> You loving them through me—
> And show them Lord You died to set them free.[3]

This is the expression of the servant's heart—of one who has humbled himself, surrendered his rights, and is willing and ready to serve his master at all costs. This is the outcome of a heart that has truly worshiped.

To Get
or to Give?

━━━━━━━━━◆━━━━━━━━━

I am not worshiping God because of what He will do for me, but because
of what He is to me. When worship becomes pragmatic, it ceases to be worship.
R. G. Letourneau used to say, "If you give because it pays, it won't pay."
That principle applies to worship; if you worship because it pays, it won't pay.
Our motive must be to please God and glorify Him alone.
—Warren Wiersbe in Real Worship

DEAR CHURCH,

I think this will be a difficult letter to write, for I'm not sure I can really find adequate words to express how deeply I feel about this subject. It deals with a mind-set that has become common among Christians today. It affects every area of church life, from the way we look for a church home to how we relate to a local church body. It is a mind-set that is far from what Scripture teaches, and it directly impacts corporate worship.

It is easy to see that we live in an age dominated by the spirit of commercialism and consumerism, with one feeding the other. Shopping in the Western world has become a game of multiple choice. We are bombarded daily with media influences to entice us and get us to buy the advertised product, even though there may be a dozen other products that are just as good or even better.

Tragically, the church is following the world's lead. From billboards to newspapers, churches are advertising and offering people what they hope will be unique, something that will appeal to the consumers' tastes, something they won't find in another "competing" church. The same spirit of competition that drives our Western economy now drives a large portion of the church. It seems we have forgotten that Jesus said He Himself would build His church. And so, "church shoppers" (meaning Christians) look for church homes that are to their liking, places where they will enjoy themselves—churches where the music is "their kind," where the preacher preaches the way they like a preacher to preach, and where there are programs that will take care of their children.

Many Christians today see the church primarily as something that is there "for them." They think of their own comfort, forgetting that *they are* the church and are called to minister to one another. They seem to be unaware that they are part of the body of Christ and that God desires to place them in a church congregation to live and function as members of a local body for its good and for His glory.

Please understand I am not saying that receiving is not a part of the Christian's life. After all, we are the recipients of the greatest gift anyone has ever received. Redemption is an act of grace on God's part. It is indeed a gift, not something we can earn in any way. As we grow spiritually, we are constantly on the receiving end of God's blessing. As we mature, however, our mind-set should change from what we can receive to what we can give. The mind of Christ, as we find described in the second chapter of Philippians, should increasingly become ours. We should become more and more aware that in God's economy, it is in giving that we receive; it is in losing that we find; it is in dying that we live.

With this in mind, suppose God were to lead you to a church that might not be your first choice, where you might not "get" all that, humanly speaking, you might like to get, but where your gifts and talents would be used to their optimum and where you would bring Him the greatest glory. What would you do? Obedience to Him would lead you to offer Him the highest form of worship, which is the offering of your life as a living sacrifice. When we are motivated by the mind and attitude of our Lord, our first concern in joining a church will be where God wants us to serve and where we can give the most, rather than where we can get the most.

When we moved to Atlanta a number of years ago, we felt the Lord leading us to join our lives to an inner-city church that was about to die. Although it meant a forty-mile drive each way, distance was not an issue, for we knew this was what we were to do. There were a little over one hundred people left in a church sanctuary that seated close to three thousand. Because of our ministry schedule, we could not be there as often as we would have wished, but with the time we had we placed our lives alongside those people to be available in whatever way the Lord should wish to use us. We solicited the prayers of God's people across the country, and we became quite broken over the condition of this body of believers. I wish I could report a great victory, but I can't. The church eventually closed and that prime piece of property was sold. I don't understand why. I do know, however, that we were where we were supposed to be, and through it all we learned some valuable lessons as the Lord did some major shaping in our own lives.

Some years ago, friends of ours felt God leading them to move from a church that had all the amenities one could imagine into a much smaller church. The music program was nothing compared to where they had been; it was not even the kind of music they enjoyed. There were few activities for their children; in fact, there were few children. It was the pastor's first pastorate. To the casual observer, the move didn't make sense. Friends couldn't figure out why they were doing it. The repeated question was, What did that church have to offer compared to where they had been? In terms of getting, the move was senseless. It made sense to God, however, because that was where He wanted to use them. And use them He has.

Sometimes the road up looks to others like the road down. How odd the cross appears in a world of "getters." Contrast the "get" mentality of our day with what our Lord said about following Him: "If anyone desires to come after Me, let him deny himself, and take up his cross daily, and follow Me. For whoever desires to save his life will lose it, but whoever loses his life for My sake will save it" (Luke 9:23–24).

Contrast the "get" mentality with the New Testament's teaching on being a part of a church body: "Just as each of us has one body with many members, and these members do not all have the same function, so in Christ we who are many form one body, and each member belongs to all the others. We have different gifts, according to the grace given us. If a man's gift is prophesying, let him use it in proportion to his faith. If it is serving, let him serve; if it is teaching, let him teach; if it is encouraging, let him encourage; if it is contributing to the needs of others, let him give generously; if it is leadership, let him govern diligently; if it is showing mercy, let him do it cheerfully" (Rom. 12:4–8 NIV).

What difference do you think it would make in our churches if we all saw ourselves as an integral part of the whole, with a responsibility to the other parts of the body?

This viewpoint was driven home to us in a very graphic way years ago in the Soviet Union. It was our first time to minister in a Communist country, and we had not known what to expect. We had heard all kinds of rumors. What we didn't expect was the impact these Christians behind that Iron Curtain would have on us.

In some of the churches we were the first free-world Christians the people had seen. We were welcomed with more Christian love and warmth than perhaps we had ever experienced. We were treated as brother and sister. We had come from a "Christian" country, with access to the Bible all our lives. We were there to encourage and to help them . . . or so we thought! Though I know the Lord blessed them through our presence, we soon learned that in their restricted world of Communism, these Christians had a grasp of basic Christianity that we in the West had lost. They possessed an awe and reverence of God, and they had an understanding of what the church was meant to be and how it was to function.

The pastor of the Baptist church in Sukumi, on the Black Sea, was in his early seventies. Out of respect for his wisdom and leadership, the church members had nicknamed him "the Baptist Bishop." Like so many others we met, he had spent his share of time in concentration camps because of his faith. Of the many experiences we could recount from that trip, memories that we shall treasure for years to come, one conversation particularly stands out in our minds because of its unusual nature.

The conversation took place around the dinner table in the pastor's home. He and the church deacons had been endeavoring for some time to lead a particular family in the church to an understanding of what it meant to be responsible members of the church body. Months before, the church leaders became aware of another family in the church that was in serious need of a certain item the family in question possessed in abundance. The pastor went to this family and advised them of the situation, then asked them, out of their plenty, to help this other family. They refused. The pastor visited them again, this time with several deacons. The family still refused to share, and the church took disciplinary measures. The pastor felt that this was going to be an important time of teaching for the whole church—teaching what Paul meant when he said, "If it is contributing to the needs of others, let him give generously" (Rom. 12:8b NIV). The pastor was very sensitive to the fact that God had given him the assignment to lead the church, and this was what he was attempting to do.

You may think it was wrong for the pastor to put pressure on this family to share with others since giving is a matter of the heart and, after all, it is a cheerful giver that pleases God. Yet this incident shows the seriousness these believers placed on obedience to God's instructions about serving one another. It relates directly to the matter we are discussing—what it means to be a part of a church body—and clearly illustrates the contrast between a "getting" and a "giving" mentality.

Just a few days later, in Minsk, we were asked by the assistant director of the Belarus Baptist Convention if there were people in the churches of America who were out of work. We replied that from time to time there were those who would be jobless. Then came this unexpected question: "Do the members of your churches always take care of their brothers and sisters when they have needs like that? Do they find work for them?" I hedged a bit, not having anticipated the question. I said that I was sure there were churches that felt this kind of responsibility toward their members, but I didn't think it was a general practice. I soon learned the question was asked because these were the simple, basic things that concerned them. Though they didn't have the problem with joblessness under Communism, there were other needs, and they were trying to align themselves with the teachings of Scripture in regard to the caring for one another in the body. They read that they were to be a caring, giving community of faith, and they were attempting to be obedient to their Lord. They observed in Scripture that believers were to be first of all *givers*, because of what they had been given in Christ. True worship, after all, is giving, and giving is worship. Worship is an offering, and all sincere offering is worship.

Isaac Watts expressed it so beautifully for us in this verse:

> Were the whole realm of nature mine
> That were an offering far too small.
> Love so amazing, so divine,
> Demands my soul, my life, my all![1]

Although our hymnals today for some reason use the word *present*, Isaac Watts' original word was *offering*. God isn't looking for a present; He requires an offering. He is waiting for those whom He has redeemed to offer Him a "living sacrifice." Acceptable worship requires a living sacrifice. "And Abraham built an altar there and placed the wood in order; and he bound Isaac his son and laid him on the altar" (Gen. 22:9). Identity with Christ is the key. Identity with Him in His death, so that we can offer Him the living sacrifice of our lives. This is worship!

I want to close this letter with this story, for I believe it illustrates a serious problem in the church today. The service had just concluded, and several people were sharing with me what the Lord had done in their lives that morning. The minister of music brought a young lady by to meet me. This was one about whom he had spoken to me earlier, the one with the "gorgeous voice." Just that week she had joined the church in order to be in his choir.

After we had talked for a few minutes, the young lady left, and he went on to tell me about the wonderful crop of soloists he had in his choir of several hundred. There were so many, in fact, that, except during pageant season, they only got to sing a solo in church about once a year. His music program was continually attracting musicians and singers from churches all across the city. They were joining because of all the exciting things being offered.

I restrained myself from saying what I wanted to say, mainly because there were others standing there, but my mind went immediately to the passage in 1 Samuel 12. I thought of the story the prophet Nathan recounted to King David—that of the one ewe lamb, owned by the poor man. This single lamb was taken by the rich man, who possessed a large number of sheep and cattle, and used to feed his guest. Though this may not be a perfect analogy, it illustrates the spirit that has entered the church today—a spirit that is the antithesis of the spirit we see in the early church.

You see, I knew more about the membership change by that soprano than anyone realized. I knew that in many ways she had been the "ewe lamb" in the church she had left. She had been the only trained voice in the choir. She had blessed that small congregation all year with her God-given talent. No, she didn't get to sing in any big pageants, for her congregation was small. She never experienced the thrill of participating in a choir several hundred strong. There was no orchestra to accompany her when she sang. She did a lot more giving than getting, and finally she was persuaded she would "get more out of church" if she moved. And move she did—but at what cost?

Research has shown that much of the growth of our largest churches has been at the expense of smaller churches. Much of the increase comes as a result of members from other churches being attracted to bigger and more exciting programs. I am not saying that "bigness" in itself is wrong. I am saying, however, that some vital things are being overlooked in the drive to grow bigger. Some things are being encouraged that are basically not in the Spirit of Christ. Scripture tells us when one part of the body hurts, we all hurt. When another part of the body is discouraged, we all feel it. How wrong it is when we ourselves become the source of hurt and discouragement.

That Sunday, in the small church, the "ewe lamb" was missing. "If any man would follow me. . . ."

Dear church member, remember that the Christian life is fundamentally a love relationship with God out of which issues a life of worship and service. It is a life of giving. Worship is not something you get; it is something you give! Worship does not begin in the worship service; worship begins in the heart. As the apostle Paul expressed so strongly, "I urge you, brothers, in view of God's mercy, to offer your bodies as living sacrifices, holy and pleasing to God—which is your spiritual worship" (Rom. 12:1 NIV).

PART 2

Letters to the Worship Leaders

"The Gathering"

———◆———

Coming to Him as to a living stone, rejected indeed by men, but chosen by God and precious, you also, as living stones, are being built up a spiritual house, a holy priesthood, to offer up spiritual sacrifices acceptable to God through Jesus Christ.
—*1 Peter 2:4–5*

DEAR WORSHIP LEADERS,

I want to begin this series of letters to you by examining and evaluating what I believe is a fundamental issue in the life of the church. In fact, it is so important that a current misunderstanding of it is at the root of much of the division and controversy over music and worship. I write to you about the purpose for "the gathering."

For years a gradual change has been taking place in the thinking of a large segment of the Western evangelical church regarding the primary purpose for the assembling, or gathering, of Christians. From Scripture and church history, we see that the gathering—whether in cathedrals, huts, or forests—was a meeting of the saints to worship God. At the gathering they worshiped through music, the reading of Scripture, and prayer. Messages were delivered to them out of God's Word. At the gathering they met around the Lord's table to remember His death; at the gathering they asked their questions and had fellowship with one another. These meetings were expressly for believers.

In Old Testament days as well, the gathering was always a coming together of God's people. The prophet Joel said, "*Gather* the people, Sanctify the assembly, Assemble the elders, *Gather* the children and nursing babes" (Joel 2:16,

83

italics added). Over the course of Israel's history, the people were often summoned by their leaders to hear a word from God. Sometimes these were messages of instruction or warning, and sometimes "the gathering" was for a time of corporate repentance, worship, or celebration. Whatever the purpose, the summons was to *God's people* to gather. The gathering was for a special people with a specific purpose. It was not for the world; it was for His chosen ones, and it always pertained to some aspect of their relationship with Him.

During the days of our Lord's ministry, He was often followed by large crowds attracted to Him by His miracles. He did not invite the crowds, however, to join Him when He taught the profound truths of His kingdom. His gatherings were for His disciples. "And seeing the multitudes, He went up on a mountain, and when He was seated His disciples came to Him. Then He opened His mouth and taught them" (Matt. 5:1–2).

The gathering on the mountainside was a specific time for Jesus' disciples to meet with Him for teaching. Have you ever wondered why, when He was about to deliver such an incredible sermon as this one "on the mount," He did not choose to teach it to as large a crowd as possible? Why was it directed to the disciples? Why wasn't everyone invited? Wasn't there a chance that, if the crowd had been invited, the Lord would have gained more followers? Was Jesus' exclusion of the crowds an indication that He was not interested in evangelism? We know this was not the case, for He had come to seek and to save those who were lost. Yet there were regular times when He was not seeking them. Those were the times He met alone with His disciples for their instruction and edification.

In His message to His disciples during this same gathering on the mountain, Jesus told them that they were the salt of the earth and the light of the world (Matt. 5:13–16). The earth and the world represented the hopelessness and darkness of those without Christ. Jesus was telling the disciples that they were to leave the "mountainside gathering," where they had been nurtured and taught, to go out into the darkness bearing the light. He was teaching them that "going" followed the "gathering." He was telling them that the gathering is not complete in itself but finds its completion in the going.

"When He had come down from the mountain, great multitudes followed Him" (Matt. 8:1). The meeting was over now, and the service began. Except for the blocks of time He regularly spent communing with His Father and the private teaching times with the disciples, Jesus and His followers were speaking and ministering to those in need. They "went to the world."

When going does not follow the gathering, we have an incomplete, introverted Christianity. Conversely, if we fail to understand the need and purpose for the gathering, we end up with weak evangelism. Without the support, edification, challenge, and strength derived from the gathering, the going will be in the power of the flesh. The light will be dim and ineffective, and the salt will have little savor.

We find this principle of gathering and going continued in the Book of Acts. Since the Day of Pentecost, the regular corporate meeting of the church was a meeting of and for believers. The first actual gathering was at the instruction of our Lord when He commanded them not to leave Jerusalem, but to wait for the gift the Father had promised. "When the Day of Pentecost had fully come, they were all with one accord in one place. And suddenly there came a sound from heaven, as of a rushing mighty wind, and it filled the whole house where they were sitting" (Acts 2:1–2). Immediately after they were filled and empowered by the Holy Spirit they "went out into the city," and the world took notice that they were different: "So they were all amazed and perplexed, saying to one another, 'Whatever could this mean?' . . . But Peter, standing up with the eleven, raised his voice and said to them . . . " (Acts 2:12, 14).

The church was making its debut in the world—a debut immediately preceded by the gathering in the upper room. We see this pattern continuing throughout the New Testament—believers gathering, then going. We find the believers gathered in Acts 4 when Peter and John joined them upon their release by the Jewish leaders. We hear God's people praying together, and we watch as they leave to go back into the world—refilled, equipped, empowered by the Holy Spirit, speaking the Word of God boldly. Gathering and going, gathering and going, gathering to worship, pray, fellowship, break bread together, to be instructed and equipped to go. This is the recurring picture we see of the New Testament church. They gathered, then went out to evangelize.

Much of the message of the epistles had to do with the church *gathered*. It was during the gatherings that these letters were read. This was when the early church was taught who they were in Christ and what their assignment was. It was the time when they learned how they were to interact with God and with one another. It was a time when they were taught how they were to relate to the world. It was that moment in the week set aside for the believers to meet. There was no hidden agenda or ulterior motive. It was for them! It was not for evangelizing, it was not for the unbeliever; it was for the church. It was a picture, in miniature, of that glorious and final "gathering" seen by John—that "great multitude which no one could number, of all nations, tribes, peoples, and tongues, standing before the throne and before the Lamb" (Rev. 7:9).

I am writing this letter to you, Worship Leaders, out of a conviction that this is an area we need to examine carefully in light of what we find in Scripture. What do you see as the reason for the gathering? From what the Bible portrays, a definition might be as follows:

> The Gathering (the church assembled): a time for God's people to pray, worship, fellowship with one another, to be edified, nurtured (fed and strengthened in their faith through the preaching and teaching of Scripture), and equipped (instructed in the ways of being light and salt in the world) to live in the world while not being conformed to it (not being pressed into its mold, not being changed *by* it while effecting change *in* it).

For much of the evangelical church in North America, the gathering for believers has increasingly become a gathering for evangelization. No longer is this primarily a time for worship and for prayer. No longer is this the time for exhorting, encouraging, and equipping the saints for the work of ministry. As a result, most Christians are ill equipped to be salt and light in their daily interactions with unbelievers. Evangelism is seen to be the function of the gathering, not the responsibility of the believer, and is often left for the pastor to do when he preaches.

A pastor friend of ours came face-to-face with this in his ministry several years ago. He had been called to a church he knew had great growth potential. Having trained pastors and churches on how to do evangelism during the years he had been associate director of evangelism for his state, he looked forward to getting on with the program. What eventually happened not only surprised him but also totally changed his life and the life of his church.

After four years of pushing for growth and majoring on evangelism, he had come to the end of his rope. He had worn himself and his people out. There was a group of people in the church wanting him to leave. He decided to give up and go back into the business world and began writing out his resignation.

That was the week of the state's annual convention. He and his wife attended the meetings and heard Henry Blackaby speak. To make a long story short, God began reshaping their lives as the two of them went through the study course *Experiencing God*. God brought them back to a basic understanding of who they were and what the church really is.

During the course of this reorientation, God asked this pastor some crucial questions. The first was, "To whom does your church belong?"

"To you, Lord," he replied.

"Then I want my church back," the Lord said.

The next question: "What are you?"

"A pastor," he replied.

"What is a pastor?" the Lord continued.

"A shepherd," came the answer.

"What does a shepherd do?"

"A shepherd takes care of the sheep, makes sure they are well fed, protects them, ministers to the ones who are sick and hurting, and goes after those who wander off," he replied.

"And what do healthy sheep do?"

"They grow wool and reproduce."

"What have you been doing these last four years?" asked the Lord. This last question pierced his heart, for it was then that he realized what had been wrong. His first concern had not been shepherding his flock; his focus had been almost exclusively on getting more sheep. He had worn himself and his flock out with his driving attitude. He had been trying to build "his" church.

After realizing what had been happening, he confessed his sin to his people and asked their forgiveness. He told them he was going to become their pastor. He was going to love them and care for them, and he would leave the results with the Lord.

He soon discovered that there were ten couples in his fold who were on the verge of divorce. He began ministering to them and, to God's glory, not one of these couples divorced. As other hurts and sicknesses surfaced, God graciously ministered healing and restoration.

During this process God was shaping the lives and character of His people. They were becoming a praying church. The pastor would phone me from time to time to report on what was happening. One Thursday he called, and I'll never forget what he said. "Ron, you won't believe this, but at the close of prayer meeting last night, seven people walked down the aisle to make public their profession of faith in Christ. I had never heard of five of them. The sheep are multiplying. For the time being, we've suspended visitation night because I'm having a hard time keeping up with the new lambs being birthed by my healthy sheep."

What this pastor friend was witnessing was the Lord adding to the church through healthy, mature sheep. These sheep were being prepared in the gathering to go out into the world and bear fruit. They didn't have to be driven to reproduce; it was the natural outgrowth of their health and maturity. And they weren't waiting for the world to come to them.

The thrust of many church outreach programs today focuses on getting the world to "come to church." Programs are developed to attract the world. The messages delivered and the invitations extended at the gathering are often directed primarily, if not exclusively, to the lost. On those occasions when the message happens to be directed to believers, even then, the appeal often focuses exclusively on the lost person or on the nonmember Christian in attendance. The "go to them" of the New Testament has become the "come to us" of today's church.

This is not to say that every service must be a worship service or must be exclusively for believers. There are different kinds of meetings, and some of these are primarily evangelistic, as they should be. The problem is that many see *every* meeting as a time for evangelism, leaving no time for the gathering of the church to worship, equip, fellowship, and grow.

But suppose there are unbelievers present during the regular worship service of the church. Shouldn't there be an evangelistic message and call presented? Otherwise, they will not have an opportunity to come to Christ. According to Scripture, this argument does not hold true. In 1 Corinthians 14, the apostle Paul made clear that when the church is gathered to worship, if an unbeliever happens to be present, he will be "convinced by all" and "convicted by all. And thus the secrets of his heart are revealed; and so, falling down on his face, he will worship God and report that God is truly among you" (vv. 24–25). When the church is truly worshiping, the power of the Holy Spirit is sufficient to bring people to salvation. We see the reality of this demonstrated during the Welsh Revival of 1904–1905, when there was very little, if any, preaching to the lost. Yet during a six-month period, approximately one hundred thousand people came to Christ.

When our church evangelism programs revolve around getting the world to "come to us," we'll go to almost any means to accomplish this. We find out from the world the kind of music they like, and we adjust the music of the gathering accordingly. We discover that symbols such as the cross are offensive to the world, so we remove them. Since we are trying to make the world feel at home when they come to church, we present the gospel in the form of entertainment. The world responds to this nondemanding, entertaining atmosphere; and before you know it, the worship center that had become an evangelistic center has evolved into a theater. We have only to look at the architectural structure of many church buildings being built today to see this is true. They are designed as theaters, and some churches now rival the world in their theatrical productions. (See "When Church Was Just Church" in the Appendix.)

"The Gathering" is no longer what God intended it to be. In many cases, it has lost its purpose and meaning. I write to you, Church Leaders, so that you will not get caught up in this kind of thinking. I pray that you will follow hard after that which God called you to be—those who edify and equip the saints. The apostle Paul said, "Him we preach, warning every man and teaching every man in all wisdom, that we may present every man perfect in Christ Jesus. To this end I also labor, striving according to His working which works in me mightily" (Col. 1:28–29). Guard your hearts from getting sidetracked. I write to you, worship leaders, that you will faithfully fulfill your calling by leading your gathering to an encounter with God that will build them up in the faith and equip these chosen ones, these people belonging to God, that they might faithfully declare the praises of Him who called them out of darkness into His glorious light (paraphrased from 1 Peter 2:9). I pray that the following letters will be of some help and encouragement to you.

The Pastor's Role as Worship Leader

———————◆———————

The assignment of the worship leader is to keep the congregation's focus on God, the object and subject of all true worship.

DEAR PASTOR,

In recent years we have witnessed a phenomenal growth, as well as change, in Christian music ministry, both in and out of the church. This growth has resulted in music becoming more important than it ought to be in some churches. More and more it is becoming the major driving force of the meeting time or the gathering. If it were not for the music, specifically a certain *kind* of music, some churches would lose many of their members. Some shop for and join churches primarily for the music. It has become so important, in fact, that in recent years the director of music has even been given the title of *"worship leader," "pastor of worship and celebration,"* or some such designation.

There are those churches where it is the music director alone who plans the service, picks out the hymns, and so on. There are many churches where the pastor gives little or no input into the order of service. All these things come under the assignment of the director of music, for he is the one considered the worship leader.

As I will point out to you in my next several letters, worship is so much more than music. In fact, you don't have to have music to worship. I am not saying that music cannot play an important part in the act of worship. I am saying, however, that its importance has been greatly overemphasized. It has become so important that in many people's minds, the music part of the service is when they believe worship takes place, and the rest of the service falls under some other category.

I am writing this letter to say, Pastor, that you, as the one who has been given the responsibility to shepherd the flock God has put under your care, are the principal worship leader. It has been given to you, as the shepherd, to oversee what takes place when your people gather to worship. It is your responsibility to see that they are given every opportunity to have a genuine worship encounter with God, one that will result in some lasting change and a deeper walk with Him. If you have a director of music with whom you work, then as a team you need to pray together, plan together, and minister together as worship leaders.

Some pastors today have abdicated their worship leading role and, other than knowing what they will be preaching on and who will be praying, have no idea what will happen in the service. They don't know the content of the music special—choir or solo—that will be sung before they preach, and they have not discussed what might be the most appropriate invitation or closing hymn that would tie in with their message.

I am not advocating that the pastor so control the planning of a service that he quenches the inspiration and leadership of the Holy Spirit working through others, such as the director of music. The pastor's role should not be one of control but one of oversight and involvement. Perhaps God has placed someone on your staff who is especially gifted and sensitive in the area of worship preparation. If so, be grateful and allow this person the freedom to express the gifts God has given him in this area. The main thing is that you work together as a team in planning the worship, with each one listening to and showing respect for the other. When time has been spent praying together, the same Spirit who is at work in each one will guide and bring unanimity to the planning and preparation. Then when all are gathered to worship, the worship facilitators will be united in heart, mind, and spirit, ready and available to meet God in worship with their people. (For further information, see the "Checklist for Worship Leaders" in the Appendix.)

Pastors, as worship leaders, you are responsible before God for the way you lead those entrusted to your care in worship. I urge you to take this assignment seriously and to make every effort to do those things that please the heart of God and lead your people to an encounter with Him.

The Primacy of Prayer in Worship

Prevailing prayer is God's ordained means for extending His kingdom, for defeating Satan and his empire of darkness and evil, and for fulfilling God's eternal plan and bringing into effect His good will on earth.
—*Wesley Duewel*

DEAR PASTOR,

In an earlier letter to you I told you about some of the memorable experiences we had in churches in the former Soviet Union. To our surprise, we discovered that our brothers and sisters in Christ had an understanding of and commitment to the essentials of the Christian faith that many of our churches in the West had allowed to be crowded out by nonessentials. One of the many surprises was that prayer played such an important role in the life of these churches. Having read that Jesus said His house was to be called a "house of prayer," these believers called their meeting places "prayer houses." Not only did they have regular corporate prayer meetings, but each time they met to worship, a significant portion of those three-hour services was devoted to prayer by the pastor/leaders and by the people. We have also found this same devotion to prayer evident in other parts of the world where we have ministered.

This, however, cannot be said of the Western church. It seems that over the years more and more time has been given to programs, leaving less time for prayer. It seems the more we excel in man's mechanics, the less we know of God's dynamics. Programs and prayer were never meant to be mutually exclusive, yet we have allowed this to happen. I know of very few churches in North America that could genuinely be called "prayer houses."

In recent months I have been asking two questions relating to prayer that seem to be having a deep impact on those to whom I speak. I don't recall where they originated, but I do know we need to be asking them of ourselves and our churches today. The first one is this: *Is my personal prayer life commensurate with (equal to) the assignment I feel God has given me to be light and salt in my world?* The second is: *Is the prayer life of my church commensurate with (equal to) the assignment and vision God has given us to reach our community and beyond with the gospel?* These are sobering questions. Yet if they cannot be answered in the affirmative, how can we hope to accomplish the task God has given us?

At the end of His earthly ministry, our Lord was able to say He had brought glory to His Father by completing the work He had been given to do. One of the main reasons He could say this was that He had diligently guarded and maintained communion in prayer with His Father. In spite of the pressing needs He faced each day, He always set aside blocks of time to spend with the Father. "So He Himself often withdrew into the wilderness and prayed" (Luke 5:16).

Today, the prayer movement is one of the fastest-growing movements in the church. There are more prayer ministries than ever before. There are "prayer summits" and "prayer concerts." There are "prayer walks" and "prayer blocks." There are twenty-four-hour "prayer chains," and numerous videos and cassettes are available which present many different aspects of prayer. There are journals and magazines that focus on prayer. Though all of this may be helpful and is surely a sign of God's activity in heightening the awareness of the need for more prayer in the life of the church, the fundamental question still must be, *Is my church a house of prayer?*

Over the last several years, I have become increasingly interested in observing the content of the worship services of churches where we have been, especially the amount of time actually given to prayer. At one point I began recording the time spent in prayer as well as the time devoted to other things in the services. A time comparison revealed that four out of five churches spent more time in welcoming the visitors in a service than in all the praying combined. Two out of five of these same churches spent more time making the announcements than they did in prayer.

Dear Pastor, *if it is worship time, it is time to pray.* It is a time in which we should be speaking to God and hearing from Him. It is a time of confession and communion. In the apostle Paul's instruction to Timothy, he said: "I desire therefore that the men pray everywhere, lifting up holy hands" (1 Tim. 2:8). And remember our Lord's own words in Luke 19:46: "It is written, 'My house is a house of prayer,' but you have made it a 'den of thieves.'"

Recently my wife Patricia and I were in one of this country's largest churches. To our surprise, a total of *forty-five seconds* was spent in prayer in the Sunday morning worship service. Yet in that same service, ten minutes was allotted to an amusing video Sunday School promotion.

We say we believe in prayer. We have it listed in our church bulletins, but do we pray? If the time actually spent in corporate prayer in our worship services is an indication, we have reason to be concerned. Might a lack of prayer be the major reason that, in spite of having better programs than ever before, in spite of having bigger and fancier buildings than ever, in spite of there never before being so many megachurches, we are making less impact on society than ever before? Could prayerlessness be the reason the darkness in our land is becoming increasingly dark? Could it be that the prayerlessness of our churches is why so many are powerless?

There are Christians today who seem to be more interested in getting prayer back in our schools than back in our churches. Many who petition, picket, and lobby for school prayer show little interest in attending a prayer meeting or starting one in their church. *The reason we do not still have prayer in the public schools of our land is that prayer has ceased to be a priority in our churches.* In many of our current religious "causes," we spend our time and money dealing with symptoms rather than with the root problem. If the soundness of the root system is not restored, no amount of time spent working on the branches is going to produce healthy fruit.

Pastor, if it is time to worship, *it is time for prayer in the pulpit.* Though there are exceptions, the pulpit prayer—or what some call the invocation or pastoral prayer—is no longer given the place of importance it once had in the evangelical churches of North America. As a lad growing up in Canada and Switzerland, I had the privilege of hearing weekly the pulpit praying of my father. The impression I formed was that this was a very important moment in the service. I thank God for this heritage, as well as for the blessing of being teamed in ministry over the years with men who believed speaking to God in the hearing of their people was a very serious matter. We have often heard Dr. Stephen Olford speak about the amount of time he gave to preparing his own heart for that moment when he stood before his people and talked to God. He described the time it took to consider the Scriptures he might use and to observe those events happening in the world, the community, the church family, that needed to be brought to God in prayer when the "family" gathered. He went so far as to encourage pastors to make notes of what needed to be addressed in prayer.

Charles Haddon Spurgeon, the great British preacher of another generation whose sermons are still being read and "repreached" by thousands of ministers today, admonished the young pastors of his day to outline their "pulpit prayers." Those who knew Spurgeon personally knew him as being as powerful in prayer as he was in preaching.

Dr. Martyn Lloyd-Jones, with whom it was our privilege to be teamed in ministry for a week in the late 1960s, was known by many as much for his praying as his preaching. Vernon Higham, one of Lloyd-Jones's closest friends, told me recently of a visit he made to see Mrs. Lloyd-Jones some months after her husband's death. They talked of how much they missed his preaching, at which point she said, "But I miss his praying more!" I do not recall the topic of Dr. Lloyd-Jones's sermons the week we were together, but I do recall the impact his praying had on all of us. Each time he finished, we hoped nothing would happen for a while because we had been led into the very throne room of God.

Dr. Olford tells of an experience he had when pastoring in the London area during the period of Lloyd-Jones's ministry at Westminster Chapel. He and his wife Heather had a free weekend and went to Westminster Chapel to worship. Having heard of the time and importance Lloyd-Jones gave to his pulpit praying, Dr. Olford decided to check the length of that morning's prayer. It was twenty-two minutes long! Twenty-two minutes of talking to God! Not only does twenty-two minutes sound extreme in our day, but it would be tantamount to prodding the deacons to call an emergency meeting to meet with the pastor to discuss his future! We don't have time for that much praying! Isn't that much too long? It does seem so when compared to the brief prayer that is so often offered, thanking God for the good weather, the opportunity to again be assembled, and asking Him to bless the service. *If it is worship time, pastor, it is time for you to pray.*

If it is worship time, it is also time for your people to pray. In many evangelical circles, the only time the worshipers are given an opportunity to express anything is when they sing. Everything else is done for them by those "up front." Our people have become so accustomed to this that they often feel strange when asked to do anything else, such as give a testimony or participate in corporate prayer. Yet if they are there to worship, they would surely benefit from other ways of expressing themselves to God. Since the role of a worship leader is to assist the people in meeting God and saying to Him what they need to say, how best to accomplish this should be at the heart of the prayerful planning of each worship service. *If it is worship time, it is time for the people to pray!*

How wonderful it would be if, when a pastor looked at his congregation on a Sunday morning, he knew in his heart he was looking at a sea of praying people. Rather than being the rule today, however, this would be the exception. In most of our churches, a call for public prayer is an uncomfortable moment for many of our members. When a service is opened up to a time of spontaneous prayer, more often than not there is an awkward period of silence. One of the reasons is that many people spend so little time verbalizing prayers in private that when it comes to praying in church, they are not sure what to say.

How do we help them? What can we do to engage the congregation in acts of prayerful participation? It will take prayer on your part, Pastor, to find ways to break your people of what often is "people fear." Teaching people to pray will take wisdom, time, instruction, and patience, but it can and must be done if we are really to become the people God desires us to be. I have a few suggestions that may help. But in the final analysis, God is the One who will direct you to do what is best in your situation as you lead your people from where they are to where God wants them to be.

In addition to the usual three times listed in church bulletins (beginning, offering, and end) you might consider setting a block of time aside in each worship service to have one or two of your people pray. This could be done around the offering, or before or after the Scripture reading. Whenever it is, it needs to be a time when someone from the congregation prays. Include your young people. I would recommend that you notify those you will ask to pray in advance so they can be thinking and preparing themselves for that important moment in worship. It may be that you, Pastor, will need to help them, teaching them how to use Scripture in their prayers (praying back to God what He has said and promised). Let them know it is not offensive to the Lord to make notes of what they want to pray about. This can turn out to be a significant tool for spiritual growth among your people—not just the youth, but the congregation as a whole.

Another way to move your people from spectator mode to participatory mode is to ask them to repeat a prayer after you, phrase by phrase. This can be a moment of spontaneous prayer, or perhaps a prayer out of Scripture. Whatever it is, you are helping your people to say those things to God they need to say if they are going to worship Him. In actuality, this may be the only real praying some of your people will do all week long, other than thanking God for their food at mealtime.

Finally, let me suggest something that may seem unfamiliar to some of you. I've seen the Lord use this, however, in a very significant way in more and more churches as congregations are actually learning to pray *together.* Think about prayerfully preparing a prayer for your people to pray, giving them the words they need to say to God. I am not suggesting that you necessarily do this in every worship service, for—like anything else—it could become meaningless if overdone. Remember, however, we are endeavoring to lead the people beyond just singing songs and hearing sermons to an encounter with God. Remember also that Jesus said His house was to be a "house of prayer."

The following is an example of a corporate prayer that includes much Scripture. It is a prayer that could be prayed in the early part of the service as "heart preparation." Helping the people prepare their hearts for worship is vital since many, if not most, make no preparation themselves. They arrive spiritually cold and are seldom given the opportunity to think about what they are there to do. As worship leaders, we need to help them prepare their hearts to offer God acceptable worship. (This prayer may be copied in full or in part for worship service use.)

Congregational Prayer

Sovereign God, we live in a world made sick and sad by the effects of sin. Our minds and our senses have been bombarded with news of violence and corruption, with distracting thoughts, and with the duties and demands of our lives. Help us in these moments to get quiet and still before You. Help us to hear what You would say to us.

You are the light of the world. Shine into my heart and life, overcoming any darkness You find there. Grant me the desire to hear You speak and the willingness to let You work changes in me. Touch my spiritual eyes that I may see You as You are—high and holy, majestic in Your glory—yet also near to those who are humble and contrite in spirit.

O God, You spoke of Yourself to Moses as being "the Lord, the compassionate and gracious God, slow to anger, abounding in love and faithfulness, maintaining love to thousands, and forgiving wickedness, rebellion and sin." Speak those words anew to my heart, and help me honestly to acknowledge and humbly confess my sins to You. For You resist the proud but give grace to the humble.

You have said that Your thoughts are higher than our thoughts, Your ways higher than our ways. Father, we confess that we too often have neglected Your Word, and we have failed to seek to learn Your ways and listen to Your thoughts. Lord Jesus, You have said that apart from You we can do nothing. Forgive our sinful, foolish thinking when we think we can live independently from You. Lord, I admit that I am utterly dependent upon You.

Some of us, O God, have come to this moment with urgent needs, some with deep sorrow, some with physical or emotional problems, some with family crises, others with perplexing questions. We need and ask You for help and mercy. Our hope is in You. Bring to our remembrance the promises of Your grace and strength which You have given to those who love You and trust in You.

Graciously help us now to focus on You. Help us to put away every competing thought, and with sincerity of heart to worship You— Father, Son, and Holy Spirit. We pray this in the name of our great Savior, Jesus. Amen.

The Importance of Scripture Reading in Worship

◆

Your word is a lamp to my feet
And a light to my path. . . .
Your testimonies I have taken as a heritage forever,
For they are the rejoicing of my heart.
—Psalm 119:105, 111

DEAR PASTOR,

In his first letter to Timothy, his son in the ministry, the apostle Paul stressed the importance of reading Scripture publicly when the church gathered (1 Tim. 4:13). This is an admonition we need to take to heart today because this is an area of serious deficiency in many of our churches. As our services have become shorter and we have given more time to other things, there has been little time left for any substantial reading of Scripture. Often the only Scripture read during the gathering is the few verses read by a pastor before he preaches.

The reading of the Word of God no longer holds a central place in the worship services of many churches in North America. We still say we love God's Word and base our lives on it, but if we gauge our love and commitment by the amount of time we give to reading it when we gather as God's people, there is reason to question our claim. When is the last time you heard an entire chapter read during the gathering? We say there just isn't enough time.

We do have time, however, for other things. Recently I attended a Sunday morning worship service in which a full *thirty minutes* was given to music. There were four "specials," one hymn, and six different choruses, each repeated a number of times. Since the length of the service was limited to approximately an hour, there was only time for the reading of *two verses* from the Bible.

Some have said that Paul's admonition to read Scripture publicly is not as applicable in our day because everyone has a Bible to read, whereas those in the early church did not personally have the Scripture and depended on its being read to them. This may sound logical, until you ask how many of your people are actually regularly reading the Bible. The only Scripture many will hear or read all week long will be when they are in church. This is God's Word. This is God speaking to us! The enemy trembles when he hears it, for he has no defense against it. Why is it, then, that we give so little time to its reading when we gather?

Pastor, in addition to hearing you reading God's Word from the pulpit, your people need to be reading it themselves. As the apostle Paul said, "All Scripture is given by inspiration of God, and is profitable for doctrine, for reproof, for correction, for instruction in righteousness, that the man of God may be complete, thoroughly equipped for every good work" (2 Tim. 3:16–17).

Some churches incorporate portions of Scripture from both the Old and New Testaments into their worship to be read by members of the congregation. This is an effective way to include both your older members and your young people. Passages should be assigned a week or more in advance in order for them to have time to practice the reading. It will take time to plan, and it will take time in the worship service. It may mean that, unless you lengthen the worship service, you will have to cut out some other things. You may have to rearrange the order of worship priorities.

Another way to involve your people in the reading of Scripture is to call on everyone to read a passage simultaneously. Because of the many translations used today, you will need to print the portion of Scripture in your bulletin or on an insert, unless your church has pew Bibles. The passages could be projected on overheads, if you routinely use a projector. Should you choose to use the responsive reading section of your hymnal, let me encourage you to have *everyone* read *every verse*. When the reading is done responsively, many times the congregation pays more attention to making sure they don't read the leader's print than to what the verses are really saying. I believe the people not only need to be listening to the Word, but they need to be hearing themselves speak it.

There are times when an explanation of the setting of the Scripture to be read can bring the passage to life. A preliminary word about the author, the people, or church to which it was written, or the reason it is relevant to us today can make the difference between just reading Scripture and its speaking to the hearts of those who are reading.

Pastor, remember that your role as shepherd and worship leader is to lead your people to God and help them respond to Him. The reading of God's Word must be given the prominence it requires in worship if we are going to worship in spirit and in truth, for His Word is truth!

The Priority of Preaching in Worship

By "exposing" the truth of the Scriptures and praying for the Holy Spirit's enabling,
preachers can exercise the art, science, and spiritual gift of preaching.
And by understanding the preacher's exceptional role as a mouthpiece for God,
they can live an exemplary life, dedicated to serving Christians and non-Christians alike.
—Stephen F. Olford

DEAR PASTOR,

Recently at the beginning of a *Return to Worship* seminar, a pastor shared with me that he now had less than twenty minutes to preach on Sunday mornings because more time was needed for "worship." He said the music portion of the service was expanding, and now that a drama skit was being included each week something had to be cut. They had mailed out a survey to the church membership. The question was: Which would you prefer: (1) add fifteen minutes to the service? (2) decrease the "worship" time? (3) shorten the sermon? The majority chose to have a shorter sermon.

As we analyze this, several things surface. First of all, this is not a unique situation for a pastor in America. It is, rather, a picture of church today, both from the standpoint of the leadership and of the people. The people want to be entertained, and the church leadership is willing to oblige. If the people want more music and drama, we will give it to them. Today music and drama will win hands down over preaching in many of our churches.

Secondly, in this situation there was a disorientation on the part of the pastor and people as to what worship is. This is an example of what I have talked about in another letter; many view the music portion of the service as being the worship time, while the rest of the service is something else. They do not see preaching, prayer, and Scripture reading as worship.

Thirdly, this church did not understand that worship is essentially a response to God's Self-revelation in Scripture and that, in the context of worship, preaching is God speaking to His people through His Word. One of the outgrowths of the Reformation was the restoring of the priority of preaching to the church. This was visibly evidenced by the returning of the pulpit to the center of the platform.

Pastor, when your people gather, they need to hear from God. They have been hearing all sorts of messages all week long; they now need to hear a message from His Word. As important as it is for them to have time to express themselves to God, it is more important that they hear God express Himself to them; that they be fed from His Word; that they be instructed in the ways of God's kingdom; that they be effectively strengthened by His might in their inner beings to be salt and light to the world in which God has placed them.

The apostle Paul emphatically instructed Timothy, his son in the ministry, to *preach the Word:*

> All Scripture is given by inspiration of God, and is profitable for doctrine, for reproof, for correction, for instruction in righteousness, that the man of God may be complete, thoroughly equipped for every good work. I charge you therefore before God and the Lord Jesus Christ, who will judge the living and the dead at His appearing and His kingdom: Preach the word! Be ready in season and out of season. Convince, rebuke, exhort, with all longsuffering and teaching. For the time will come when they will not endure sound doctrine, but according to their own desires, because they have itching ears, they will heap up for themselves teachers; and they will turn their ears away from the truth, and be turned aside to fables (2 Tim. 3:16–4:4).

Pastor, the call God has placed on your life as a shepherd is to, first of all, feed your sheep. Remember this:

> We've a gospel to preach, we've a message to share,
> God's eternal Word is what we declare.
> It's the power to save, it's the Spirit's sword,

It's the heart of God, it's the living Word.
We must study to learn and not be ashamed
To proclaim God's truth in the Savior's name;
With no compromise, but consistently,
We must preach the Word with integrity.

What is made by man will one day be gone,
But God's Holy Word marches on and on.
Though the flower will fade and the grass will die,
His eternal Word ever will abide.
We must pay the price, we must take our stand,
With a heart on fire and God's Word in hand;
On the brightest day, in the darkest hour,
We must preach the truth in the Spirit's power.

As a steward I must watch how I live day and night,
For the Word I preach must be backed by my life.
It's God's will, that is how He intends it to be;
Truth incarnate, the Word fully formed in me.
If we fail in our homes, if we fall into sin,
It will cancel out what we do for Him.
We must live pure lives, without fault or shame,
And live out the truth that we're called to proclaim.

Preach the Word, preach the Word,
Won't you purpose in your heart to preach the Word?
It's our call as His disciples to pass on what we've received;
Make up your mind and take the time to preach the Word.[1]

The Place of Music in Worship

Next to theology, I give the first and highest honor to music.
—Martin Luther

Great theology, married to great hymnology,
rises to God in great doxology.
—Stephen Olford

DEAR WORSHIP LEADERS,

The New Testament relationship of music to worship was established by our Lord when He and His disciples closed the celebrating of the first Lord's Supper with the singing of a hymn. The early church sang hymns to Christ in the catacombs. Ever since that day music has held an important place in the worship of the church. The proper use of music can enhance and encourage true worship; its misuse can hinder it. This is why we must give careful consideration to the place of music in worship.

In the context of a worship service, music should never be "music for music's sake." As worship leaders, we are there to assist the people, through the medium of music, to encounter God. We are not there just to sing and play songs. We are not there to entertain or "perform" for an audience; we are there to use everything at our disposal to glorify God and edify His people.

With this in mind, I want to share some observations I have made during over three decades of ministry in many different denominations and countries. From these observations, I will make comments and suggestions that you may find helpful as you seek to be all God desires you to be in ministering first to Him, then to the people.

1. The Rise of the Chorus and Death of the Hymn

In recent years the trend has been to de-emphasize hymns while going more and more to choruses. Many have nearly abandoned the rich hymn heritage of the church, and some no longer have hymnals to use. I believe this trend is, in many ways, like the experiments the educational leaders of our land have conducted with our students. Phonics was declared "out"; in came a "new and better way" to learn to read. As a result, we now have high-school classrooms filled with students who can't read. The "new and better way" didn't work—but it was too late to save the children on whom they had experimented.

Many churches in America are producing a generation of "hymn illiterates." Rather than learning about their great hymn heritage, our children and young people are being fed minibites of song literature and are not being given the opportunity to sink their teeth into anything substantial. Consequently, they will not know that hymns were a primary means of learning and spreading the doctrines of the church in past generations. They will not know that the great Reformer, Martin Luther, began writing hymns so his doctrine would be remembered, and that these hymns had a great deal to do with the spreading of the Reformation as groups of traveling singers went from village to village singing his hymns.

The next generation will not know anything about Isaac Watts, the father of English hymnody. They will not have learned the words, "When I survey the wondrous cross, On which the Prince of glory died, My richest gain I count but loss, And pour contempt on all my pride." Can you imagine a generation growing up never having sung, "Were the whole realm of nature mine, That were a present [an offering] far too small; Love so amazing, so divine, Demands my soul, my life, my all."

They will not know that Watts wrote 875 hymns, many of which remain in our hymnals today even though they were written more than 250 years ago. Why have they lasted so long? They have endured because they are all rooted in the doctrines of God's Word, with Jesus Christ as the central theme.

This generation, which is being denied its hymn heritage, will not know that Charles Wesley wrote thousands of hymns, and that these hymns—along with the preaching of his brother John—were used of God to bring about the Great Awakening, the revival that literally saved England from the inflammation of the French Revolution that was about to jump the English Channel.

They will never sing, "O for a thousand tongues to sing My great Redeemer's praise," or, "And can it be that I should gain an interest in the Savior's blood." They will never know the exhilaration of joining other blood-bought children of God on that magnificent refrain, "Amazing love, how can it be, That Thou my God should'st die for me."

They will not know of John Newton who, while working in the slave trade off the west coast of Africa, was gloriously saved and lived to write many hymns such as "Amazing grace! How sweet the sound, That saved a wretch like me." They will have no reference point to the scores of other writers, men and women, who down through the ages passed on the glorious truths of the gospel to the next generation. They will not know, because many pastors and directors of music of this generation have decided, in their zeal to relate to the present generation, to cut them off from their past.

Much beautiful and meaningful music has been written in recent years, and I thank God for it. Some of it—should the Lord tarry—will probably last for generations to come, unless some future generation decides they don't want anything from the past. The roots of our music heritage are deep, and it is from the deepest root systems that we receive the richest nourishment. When these roots are cut off, we deprive ourselves and others of their food. Will the generation God has given us the responsibility to nurture look back one day and wonder why we never told them about, "When peace like a river, attendeth my way, When sorrows like sea billows roll, Whatever my lot, Thou hast taught me to say, It is well, it is well with my soul." Will they wonder why they didn't grow up singing, "Crown Him with many crowns, The Lamb upon His throne," or, "Guide me, O Thou great Jehovah, Pilgrim through this barren land," to the beautiful Welsh music of *Cwm Rhondda*? Will they wonder? Will they ask why?

Pastor, Director of Music, Youth Director, if you are among those who are contributing to the death of the hymn, I appeal to you to restore the hymnal to your pews and hymns to your worship. Use the choruses, but don't deny this generation the riches of its past.

2. The Decline of Congregational Singing in the American Church

Though there are exceptions, the singing of the American church stands in sharp contrast to the singing of God's people in many other parts of the world. I have been observing this for many years and have come to the conclusion that much of the church has actually lost its song. If so, the only remedy is revival, for the problem is a spiritual one. No amount of coaxing and pumping up will have any lasting effect. You might get people to sing louder, but what good does that really do if the heart is not in it?

Although spiritual problems can only be remedied with spiritual answers, there are things that dampen the singing of even a spiritually alive church. Here are some suggestions that you may find helpful.

A. *Don't drown out the congregation with the accompaniment.* I will be writing about this in my letter to the accompanists, so I won't belabor the point here. I do want to say that when the accompanying instruments are louder than the singing, it tends to discourage the singers rather than encourage them. Often I have seen people simply standing and listening instead of participating. The accompaniment should be just that—an accompaniment.

B. *Avoid tempos that are either too slow or too fast.* The tendency in our day seems to be to sing everything extremely fast. This communicates that we must hurry and "get through" this so we can get on to the next song or the next part of the program. The speed at which we sing some hymns gives no time for the congregation to think about what they are saying. How can we sing about the holy things of God with so little thought?

C. *Don't accompany with unsingable harmonies.* Churches with creative, well-trained musicians need to be especially careful of this. Many times I've been in churches where I have wanted to sing the tenor line of a hymn but could not because the accompanist was using creative harmonies. These would have worked beautifully for a solo arrangement of the hymn, or on the final stanza as a dramatic climax, but they were inappropriate as a general accompaniment for a congregation. When this happens, the result is that the congregation is forced to sing everything in unison. This is one of the reasons we hear so little harmony in the churches of our land.

D. *Be creative in the "song service."* If you, the director of music, never do anything more than announce what will be sung and beat the tempo, there is a very real danger of boredom setting in. Don't limit your creativity to the selecting of songs that haven't been sung in a while and occasionally teaching your people a new chorus. Fresh approaches can contribute greatly to bringing life to that which would otherwise be routine. Here are a few suggestions.

—Occasionally have a unison reading of a verse. This can be read by the choir as well as the congregation. If you plan to do this, practice! Good unison reading is not easy. This could be a simple "solo" reading by the leader, one of your young people, or a child. Putting profound words on the lips of a child can be very powerful.

—Have one of the verses sung as a solo by "any of the above."

—Occasionally sing a verse or refrain a capella.

—Introduce a hymn or chorus with an appropriate Scripture, or insert Scripture within the singing of the song itself.

—Develop a medley of songs to help establish a certain truth in the minds of the people. For instance, we sometimes have the congregation sing, "Jesus, What a Friend for Sinners," but between several of the stanzas we sing a solo or duet that pertains to the subject of our Lord's love and care for us. It takes about fifteen minutes to complete the medley, but when finished it has established in the hearts and minds of the people that God's provision is complete in His Son, Jesus. Don't rush your people from one isolated topic to another. They will try to follow you, but they may end up having "just sung songs." Sometimes I take ten minutes or more with the congregation in singing "How Great Thou Art." I begin with a reading from the Psalms about the awesomeness of God, then move into "Our God Is an Awesome God," and finally into the hymn itself. After the first verse, I sometimes talk about losing our awe of and reverence for God. I use illustrations out of God's creation as a reminder of how awesome God is, then I take them to the scene in Revelation where we see the hosts of heaven worshiping the Lamb. I remind them that when we come to worship, we are not only worshiping the God of creation. We are also worshiping the God of redemption, for the God of creation is the same God who came to earth, hanged on a cross, and died. This prepares the people to sing the third stanza with a fresh awareness. Before the last stanza, I read from Revelation 22 about the return of our Lord, and close the worship experience with the chorus "Thou Art Worthy." By the time we finish, the message of that great hymn, which to many has lost its cutting edge, has again become real. All of this takes time, prayer, and preparation—but the impact is worth the effort.

—Tie hymns and choruses together. Hymns that have been sung for years can be greatly enhanced by tying them to choruses. This can also heighten the impact of the chorus. For this to happen, however, you must be careful that your selection keeps the flow of thought continuing, and that one builds on the other.

—From time to time, tell the story behind the writing of a hymn or relate a little about the life of the composer. Before or during our singing of "Amazing Grace," I sometimes talk about John Newton. This transforms the cursory singing of a song that the people had sung hundreds of times into a moment of great significance.

3. Spending More Time Singing to One Another than Singing to God

Many times, in the context of what we call a worship service, the congregation ends up singing songs of experience and testimony or songs *about* God, but little directly *to* Him. I have been in churches, both large and small, where the people never said one word to the One they had come to worship. I am not saying that songs like "Blessed Assurance," "He Lives," "I Will Enter His Gates," or "Give Thanks" do not have their place. But when we, as worship leaders, don't give the people the words they need to say *to* God when they sing, will there have been corporate worship? If the only opportunity people have to say anything in our churches is when they sing, it is especially important to choose music that verbalizes the things God is waiting to hear from worshipers who will worship in Spirit and truth.

When selecting the songs your people will be singing in a worship service, the first consideration should be the message of the words. We must make sure to include songs that address the One Who is our audience. Remember: Worship is not primarily for us; it is for Him! Let's not fail to make it so.

4. The Tendency to Treat Special Music as an Art Form

The world of entertainment has done a good job of shaping the thinking of the church in this area. Entertainment says, "You are performing a song for an audience." Whether the song is "Great Is Thy Faithfulness" or "Bring in the Clowns," it is seen as nothing more than a song to be performed. When it comes to the things of God and the church, you need to help your people see that there is a difference. Songs are not simply to be performed; they have a specific purpose and special significance.

If I were to ask you if the words of Scripture change in meaning when they are set to music, you would say, "Certainly not." If I were to ask you if a prayer ceases to be a prayer when set to music, you would give the same response. If I were to ask you, director of music, if when you are leading the congregation in a prayer to God in song, the prayer ceases really to be a prayer to God, you would say, "Of course not."

But nine times out of ten, this is what happens in this performance-and-entertainment-oriented day in which we live. Let me give you a few examples: The soloist in church on Sunday morning sings a prayer to God, such as "Great Is Thy Faithfulness." As she sings, she looks, smiles, and gestures toward the *audience in the pew.* The prayer that, without music, would have been a true prayer has now become an "art form," a song to be performed. God was not her audience, the people were. This happens every Sunday across the land—soloists, ensembles, and choirs *perform.* Most of them are probably unaware of what they are doing because their thinking is still being influenced by the world.

Even more surprising is when directors of music, in leading their congregations in songs of prayer, treat the prayer as simply a song to sing and not a prayer to God. Time and again I have seen this happen. Instead of leading the people to focus on the Lord and the words of the prayer, they themselves focus on the people, trying to get them to "sing out." I've heard them call for the repeating of a verse of a "prayer" because they knew the people could "sing it better." What was a prayer addressed to God had now been reduced to just a song to sing.

Dear Worship Leaders, it is your responsibility to teach those you work with the difference between performing and worship. You need to be constantly helping your people understand what should be happening in worship. You must continuously remind them of what they are doing and why. To do this, you yourself must understand these things. The way you lead your people in worship will be reflected in what your people understand worship to be.

Restoring *Selah* to Worship

I cannot imagine the Holy Spirit recording a word seventy-four times, then preserving
that word through all the years of
Old Testament writing and copying, just to have it
dropped in our day! The word is Selah.
—John E. Hunter

DEAR WORSHIP LEADER,

Of all the components of worship, there is one that is quite often over-looked, and may not even be considered as part of worship at all by many. Yet its presence could be the one thing that transforms a service from simply another "church meeting" into a true encounter with God. It is a missing element in much of today's worship. I'm writing to you about silence.

The day in which we live might appropriately be called "the age of noise." Those who live in an urban environment, which includes the majority of the population of North America, have noise constantly inflicted upon them. Many have become so acclimated to the cacophony of sounds which make up life that real silence is foreign to them and often makes them uncomfortable. Continuous noise has become so much a part of life that many, even when given a choice, choose noise over silence. In the home, the television blares continually; in the car, the radio or cassette player plays incessantly. Sound or noise is everywhere, leaving little time for quiet reflection.

In reality, many don't seem to miss the silence, for the constant noise keeps them from having to reflect upon their lives or to give much thought to anything but the present. This attitude is not only true of non-Christians but of Christians as well, and its influence has found its way into our times of worship. For many, silence in a worship service is uncomfortable and is to be avoided, so little time is ever given for silent reflection. We may never know what we are missing because we do not take seriously this matter of getting quiet before the Lord so we can reflect upon what He is saying to us.

I will never forget what happened at a meeting of the International Congress on Revival in Europe, during the time that I was involved in its leadership. The meeting place was high in the Swiss Alps, far away from the customary noise in which most of us live. Some of you reading this letter may very well recall that service when, following a message by a minister from England, I was not able to introduce the next speaker. The Lord had spoken so deeply through the preceding message that I just stood at the pulpit in silence. I couldn't say a thing. I couldn't even make a suggestion. I don't know how long the silence lasted, but suddenly someone began to weep. Then another began to weep. Soon, all across that congregation of Christians from over twenty countries, people were weeping.

Later that evening I was standing in the lobby of one of the conference hotels. A British pastor friend of mine came in; and when he saw me, he literally ran over, threw his arms around my neck, and began to weep. When he got his composure, I asked him what was wrong. He said, "Oh Ron, God finally got to me in the silence." He went on to explain that there were things that he had been able to avoid facing as long as he stayed busy, as long as he didn't have to get quiet. But that day God had intercepted him in the silence.

I am writing this letter to remind you that many times the "busyness" and noise of life—the constant doing and talking—can interfere with our being able to hear the voice of God speak to us. Remember Elijah's encounter with God on the mountain in 1 Kings 19 when God told him that He was going to "pass by." God sent a great and powerful wind, then an earthquake, and then a fire. But God was not in any of these. Then came a "gentle whisper," and it was in the whisper that God revealed Himself. If that were today, how many would hear God's whisper? Think of the average worship service in which something is continuously going on. Recently we were in a church service where there was not even a slight pause between any of the songs. There was constant sound for fifteen to twenty minutes, with not a moment allowed for reflection. In fact, there was little time even to take a breath. I felt "driven" from one end of the service to the other. Even during the two minutes that were set aside for the pastor, deacons, and others to kneel at the front to pray, something was happening. The piano was playing, and one of the deacons was praying aloud. There was no time at all for "reflective silence."

Dear Worship Leader, think for a moment of your own worship services. Do you ever give your people time to pause and think of what they have said to God or what He may be trying to say to them?

This is by no means a new idea. The Book of Psalms is filled with instructions to the director of music to give the people time to reflect on what they had just sung. The little word *selah*, used frequently in the Psalms, means to pause and think calmly on what has just been expressed. In the Book of Habakkuk, which was written to be sung or recited to the accompaniment of music, the prophet inserts three places to pause and reflect. Today, however, people are so unaccustomed to having time to reflect or meditate in our worship services, that if several seconds pass without something going on, they get uncomfortable and think that someone has forgotten to "do something."

In some worship traditions, a time for meditation is built into the service. This is often accompanied by quiet instrumental music and can be quite effective. But what I am thinking about even more than scheduled times of silence are those spontaneous moments, such as during the meeting in Switzerland, when, though there are other things on the agenda to do, the right thing is to pause, because the Holy Spirit is saying, "Put a *selah* here."

The Stillness of a Silent Sound

Sometimes we think we're doing well, but our hearts may be full of sin,
And little will we know how much until we get alone with Him.
Until we're able to get past the noisy questions of the head,
Until our "self" with all its claims is laid before the Lord as dead.

How can we hear God's still small voice with music blaring in our ears,
Or know the peace the Spirit brings, the touch that calms our inner
　　　fears?
Until we're willing to shut out the noisiness of life around—
Willing to wait until we know the "stillness of a silent sound."

We are afraid to get too still, for in those quiet moments we
Will have to face just what we are, something we might not like to see;
The attitudes that grieve our Lord, the pride, the failures, how we've
　　　been—
But that is why we need so much those silent times alone with Him.[1]

Making the Offering Meaningful

◆

"Bring all the tithes into the storehouse,
That there may be food in My house,
And try Me now in this,"
Says the Lord of hosts,
"If I will not open for you the windows of heaven
And pour out for you such blessing
That there will not be room enough to receive it."
—*Malachi 3:10*

DEAR PASTOR,

Once in a seminar session I was teaching, a pastor's wife asked me the question, "How can we restore meaning to the offering?" My answer seemed to startle her: "The offering will become meaningful when the offering becomes the offering again." I went on to ask her if the worship service was really the time when their members brought their tithes and offerings to the Lord, or if they basically just passed empty plates.

We spent a few minutes discussing this in the class, and I suggested that serious thought be given to making the offering a part of the corporate worship experience. One of the participants, who identified himself as a deacon, said this would be impossible to do in his church. He went on to explain that it would not work because the offering was counted during the worship service. At that point there were a few chuckles and comments from other class members, as all concluded this presented yet another issue—church leaders counting the offering when they should be worshiping. The reason for doing it this way, however, was very practical and expedient—

everything would be finished by noon, and the rest of the afternoon would be theirs.

I am writing this letter to you whose churches have fallen victim to the spirit of expediency. While not all have fallen victim, many—especially among Southern Baptists—have found it much more practical to have the tithes and offerings turned in at Sunday School. Thus, when the plate is passed in the worship service, the only things put in are the offerings of those who were not in Sunday School along with visitor or survey cards of those present.

Among my boyhood recollections of church, the memories of the offering times stand out. Since my father was a pioneer church planter, the congregations were always small. At offering time we would walk to the front and place our offerings in a basket. This, as I recall, was preceded by an explanation of the significance of what we were doing. Families would go together, though I usually went alone with the nickel or dime my parents had given me, for Dad was standing at the pulpit and Mother was at the piano. I now find it interesting that this time would have been etched in my memory. But that is history, and I could probably count on one hand the times offerings have had a similar significance to me in recent years.

Because the offering has lost its meaning in many churches, other things are often done "during the offering." It "saves time" to have the special music then, but seldom does the music have anything to do with the offering. Although we are often asked to sing at this point in the service, we don't. Instead, I usually have Patricia play something until all the offering has been received. I do this out of respect for that part of the worship service, as well as to have the full attention of the congregation for what we will be sharing.

I am writing this letter to you, Pastor, because I see this as an area in which our hearts have departed from worship. We may not see it as a need for concern, though, because we've become so accustomed to what we have substituted. In the meantime the offering, which should have so much to do with the true spirit of corporate worship, has become essentially meaningless. How can meaning be restored to the offering when it is no longer the offering?

I know of churches that have recently restored the receiving of the tithes and offerings to the corporate worship time. One church reported a significant increase in giving after doing this. But it is more than just changing the mechanics. It is more than announcing the offering and passing the plate. To make the offering meaningful again will take prayerful planning and time. But are we willing to give it the time it deserves? After hearing this suggestion in the worship seminar, one pastor began framing the offering with Scripture and corporate prayer. The offering time became a moment of soul-searching. It became a time when the worshipers were asked to stand before God, asking Him to show them anything that would hinder their offerings from being acceptable to Him.

I write this letter, Pastor, because the church today is often guilty of the sin of oversight. We do not take seriously what our Lord Himself taught: "Therefore if you bring your gift to the altar, and there remember that your brother has something against you, leave your gift there before the altar, and go your way. First be reconciled to your brother, and then come and offer your gift" (Matt. 5:23–24). If we were really obedient to this command, can you imagine what our offering times would be like? They would be times of revival. I am convinced that the key to revival is the church beginning to practice what it says it believes. When the true meaning of the offering is restored to a church, that church is on its way to being "blessable."

My prayer for you, Pastor, is that you will ask yourself if this most significant ingredient in worship has lost its meaning for you and your people. If it has, will you prayerfully consider restoring it to its rightful place in the corporate worship of your church? Will you return to worshiping the Lord with your tithes and offerings?

The Lord's Supper: A Feast of Remembrance

For as often as you eat this bread and drink this cup,
you proclaim the Lord's death till He comes.
—1 Corinthians 11:26

DEAR PASTOR,

I want to begin this letter with a look back in history to a moment that literally changed the face of the Christian world of that day. And it took place around the Lord's table.

It was on Wednesday, August 13, 1727, that the Moravian Brethren Congregation of Herrnhut met for a special communion service at the Berthelsdorf church. Times were extremely difficult for these Brethren. Many of them had endured severe persecution for their faith, and many had laid down their lives.

You may recall that the Moravian Brethren movement itself had sprung out of the martyrdom of John Huss, the great Bohemian Reformer. Now many of them had found refuge on the estate of a wealthy Christian, Count Zinzendorf. They had come from many different walks of life, with differing opinions and ways of thinking. During the early years, "harmony" would not have been the most descriptive word for this gathering of believers. But then something happened, and it began around the Lord's table that Wednesday in 1727.

God had been dealing with them about their self-will, self-love, judgmental spirits, and disobedience. As they gathered around the table that day, they were overwhelmed with a sense of their own unworthiness in light of all God had done for them. For what seemed to be the first time, they saw the wounds their Lord had endured and the blood He had shed for them. Count Zinzendorf described it this way: "O head so full of bruises, so full of pain and scorn." He went on to say that there was "a sense of the nearness of Christ" that came in a single moment to all assembled.

It is said that two of the members at work approximately twenty miles away, though unaware that the meeting was being held, became conscious of the same presence at the same moment. Some described it as another Pentecost; and, observing what was soon to happen, perhaps this is the most appropriate description, for those who met around the Lord's table that day would never be the same. In later years, Count Zinzendorf described it as a time when they did not know whether they belonged to earth or had already gone to heaven. Just as the early church had done, these believers were soon to touch their world in a way that could be explained only in terms of a revived people in the hands of their Lord. It would not be long before they would begin a twenty-four-hour prayer chain that would last for one hundred years. These Moravian Brethren would then reach out to continent after continent, people after people, with the glorious news of the saving life of Christ.

It was Moravian Brethren missionaries from Herrnhut that John Wesley observed in that storm at sea when he feared for his life. Inquiring of them why they could have such peace amid the violent storm, he was deeply impacted by their answer. Although he was on his way to convert the Indians, he was soon asking whether he himself was really converted. On his return home he would meet the Savior in a life-changing encounter and would one day be used of the Lord to bring revival and awakening to his homeland of England. Secular historians record that if it had not been for the spiritual influence of John and Charles Wesley, England would have suffered the same fate as France did during its Revolution.

As you trace the hand of God during the 1700s and into the 1800s, you see the lives of this simple, dedicated band of believers right in the middle of His activity. They were insignificant in the eyes of the world but mighty in the eyes of their Lord. At one point, this Herrnhut church that had been transformed around the Lord's table that day in August would have more missionaries on the fields of the world than all other mission groups combined.

When we look carefully at God's requirements for participating in the

Lord's Supper, we realize He has instituted into the life of the church the opportunity for His people regularly to take spiritual inventory, just as the church body did at Herrnhut. "For as often as you eat this bread and drink this cup, you proclaim the Lord's death till He comes. Therefore whoever eats the bread or drinks this cup of the Lord in an unworthy manner will be guilty of the body and blood of the Lord. But let a man examine himself, and so let him eat of the bread and drink of the cup. For he who eats and drinks in an unworthy manner eats and drinks judgment to himself, not discerning the Lord's body. For this reason many are weak and sick among you, and many sleep" (1 Cor. 11:26–30).

The Lord's Supper is, in its essence, not unlike what was called in Old Testament days a "solemn assembly" or "sacred assembly." This was an occasion when God's people assembled before Him to remember what He had done for them and to repent of their sin—individually and, more specifically, corporately as a people. This was always a very solemn moment in the life of the nation. In some circles today, however, the significance of and purpose for the Lord's Supper has been lost. This most awesome commemoration of our Lord's death that changed the life of that Moravian congregation is often tacked on to the end of a service, almost as an afterthought. Sometimes it is drowned in the festivity of an Easter extravaganza. To some, it is not much more than an event on the church calendar that shows up every quarter or so.

We were once in the home of a pastor who suddenly realized on Saturday night that the next day was Communion Sunday. He had forgotten to make the necessary arrangements, so he hastened to call several of his people, who promptly put things together. The next day they were ready—or were they? They thought they were; they acted as if they were. But I wonder what the Lord thought.

How often we go through the motions of the communion service, giving little thought to what we are doing and what it represents. With little time allotted for heart preparation, Scripture is read, a prayer is offered, the elements are taken, and out we go. Sometimes we don't even take a moment's pause to ask ourselves seriously whether we have partaken unworthily and thus are guilty of sinning against the body and blood of the Lord.

Those in the Corinthian church, to whom the apostle Paul was writing, were approaching the Lord's table just as they would any other meal, for it had lost its meaning. Today some approach the Lord's Supper as they would a meal at a fast-food restaurant. Little thought goes into its purpose or its preparation. Instead they think, *It's time to do it, so let's fit it into our already busy schedule.* Could there be any greater sin than to treat the sacrifice of our Savior so lightly?

In past generations, the partaking of the Supper was always preceded by spiritual preparation. In some parts of the world, such as Scotland, the "communion season" would actually last for several days. Not only was time given to prayer and self-examination beforehand, but following the day of communion were days of thanksgiving and worship that always included the preaching of God's Word. During one such time in 1630, at the Kirk of Shotts in Scotland, five hundred people were converted. It was the Monday thanksgiving service following communion, and the speaker was a young, unordained preacher by the name of John Livingstone. Many hours had been spent beforehand in prayer by godly men and women, and what ensued had never been seen before by those in attendance. The time which had been dedicated to commemorating the death of their Lord climaxed with hundreds finding life in Him. That encounter with God impacted the church in Scotland for years to follow.

"For this reason many are weak," the apostle Paul said to the church at Corinth (1 Cor. 11:30). I wonder, Pastor, if one of the reasons the church today is making such little impact in the world and seems to have so little power might be the careless way we treat the holy things of God? Could this be one of the reasons many of our churches are riddled with broken relationships and divorce rates equal to, and sometimes exceeding, those of the world? Could this be one explanation for the apathy toward spiritual things that is so evident among many of our members? Is our casual treatment of the Lord's Supper one reason there is so little application of the cross in the daily lives of professing Christians? The blasé attitude many in the church have toward the Lord's table—either in the lack of spiritual preparation of themselves when they do participate or the lack of conviction that this is something that they need in their lives—could this be a reason our churches are not experiencing revival?

If you are a Southern Baptist pastor in the state of Georgia, you will be familiar with *The Christian Index,* the first Baptist state paper of the Southern Baptist Convention. The following article appeared in the *Index* in the mid-1800s. In a day when the Lord's table is often approached with little sense of awe, wonder, and humility, perhaps a look back at the seriousness with which our forefathers took this holy ordinance will speak to our hearts. I pray we will be convicted as we consider the kind of preparation that was suggested— the soul-searching, repentance, making things right, and adjusting of their lives in order to line up with God's requirements. In those days, people were expected to prepare their hearts over the course of an entire week, for the commemoration of the Lord's death was a most sacred moment in their lives.

The article included twenty-four questions that Christians were to ask themselves as they prepared in advance to partake of the Lord's Supper. I want to draw your attention to seven of these. (A complete list of the questions in this article can be found in the Appendix.)

1. In the interval since last partaking of the Lord's Supper, what progress have you been making in your Christian life in proportion to the blessings of God you enjoy? Are you really gaining ground?

2. Is your love for the Savior deepening in your heart and more influential in your life?

3. Do you find that since your last commemoration of this feast of love, you have become so much more full of the Holy Spirit that you cannot only freely forgive from your heart the most unprovoked and aggravated injuries and insults, but you delight in pouring out fervent prayer on behalf of your bitterest enemy and are ready to minister to his welfare?

4. Have you expended more time and money in acts of practical benevolence to alleviate the wretchedness, and contribute to the enjoyment, both temporal and spiritual, of those whom it is in your power to help?

5. Is it more consistently your endeavor to lead to Christ those you know who have not yet met Him, and to lead those who do know Him into a closer walk with Him?

6. Since I last partook of the Lord's Supper, have I more faithfully followed the promptings of the Holy Spirit; have I listened more teachably to the slightest whisperings of His voice; have I cherished more carefully His sanctifying influences; have I guarded more jealously against the indulgence of any thought or desire that would grieve Him, or cause

Him to have to withdraw, even for a season, the manifestations of His love and the communications of His grace?

7. Do I increasingly feel it to be my highest privilege and happiness to lavish on Him every manifestation of my love; to consecrate to Him whatever I possess most precious; every gift He has bestowed, every talent He has entrusted to me; and to esteem myself honored, with the highest honor that any created being can enjoy, in being permitted to be an instrument in advancing His cause, and promoting His glory?

And so, believer, these are some points which are suggested to you for self-examination. Be assured that if you faithfully deal with your soul in this matter, by prayer, the study of the Scriptures, watchfulness, and perseverance, humbly depending on the Holy Spirit to make the Lord's Table the effectual channel it was designed to be, you will experience the divine grace from the fountain above, and the enjoyment of divine communion with the God of your salvation. Through the faithfulness of a covenant-keeping God and the power of the blessed Holy Spirit, you will be invigorated and comforted in your soul, and you will go on, in your heavenward course, progressing from strength to strength. You will continually advance in holiness, and with each successive participation in the Lord's Supper you will find yourself nearer and more ready for the sublime joy and satisfying pleasures of that world, where in the presence of a triune God, there is fullness of joy and at His right hand pleasures forevermore.

I know, Pastor, you are aware that church history records many instances of God's coming in revival blessing during the commemorating of the Lord's Supper. Is it presumptuous to think a church that faithfully and regularly examines itself and walks in obedience to God's Word will experience God's blessing? Not at all, for such a church will be in a position to be blessed. Such a church will minister in the power and boldness of the same Spirit who filled and empowered the early church. Such churches will be careful not to profane or make common those things that are holy to God, lest they forfeit those spiritual blessings promised to them in Christ Jesus. They will live with the awareness that God will only bless a "blessable" people. The Lord's Supper provides the opportunity to check up on ourselves to see whether we are blessable.

The Lord's Supper is a time of worship. In light of what we have already seen worship to be in Scripture, the Lord's table is one of the most meaningful times in the life of the church to offer God our worship. In the proclaiming of the Lord's death, we are acknowledging our own death with Him. In the remembering we process the ramifications of the cross in our own lives. In the remembering is a returning to the Lord. In the remembering is a fresh surrender. In the remembering is the presenting of our bodies as living sacrifices, holy and acceptable to God which is, as Paul wrote to the church in Rome, *"your spiritual worship"* (Rom. 12:1 NIV).

The table itself serves as an altar. It portrays the sacrifice of our Lord, and it invites us to a new level of sacrifice. It calls us again to die to self, take up our cross, and follow Him.

> *This place, oh Lord, the altar. The offering? my life!*
> *My body, Lord, I give to You, a living sacrifice.*
> *Lord, I surrender all my rights, my will, my talents, too.*
> *Lord, not a thing would I hold back, I yield my all to You.*[1]

The Lord's Supper is family time. The supper our Lord had with His disciples was as intimate a family time as ever has been, as He shared that last meal with those closest to Him, His "family." The Lord and His disciples were remembering the Feast of the Passover when He took the bread, blessed and broke it, and gave it to them, saying, "Take, eat; this is My body" (Matt. 26:26). They were remembering that night in Egypt when God instructed His people to kill a spotless male lamb and sprinkle the blood over the top and down the sides of their doors. They then went into their homes and ate the meat of the lamb together, as families. The first Passover was a family time.

When the church gathers to commemorate the Lord's death, it is a family gathering. There is no other moment in the life of the church when members of the family ought to feel closer to one another than when they are at the Lord's table, remembering His death. But just as the experience of sharing a family meal at home is becoming less and less the norm in our society, so the communion at church has lost its importance. Many of our churches today are losing the sense of the corporate experience of the Supper, as most of the family don't even bother to attend. And for those who do attend, we seldom share a common loaf or cup anymore. We're given separate pieces of bread or an individual wafer. Some churches now even "deliver" the bread and juice in a "combo-cup." This takes less time and is said to be more efficient. Dear pastor, have we departed so far that we now look at the Lord's Supper the same way we look at getting a burger and drink at MacDonalds? Has the meaning of the Supper been swallowed up in the name of expediency?

In the rush of contemporary living, it is more important than ever that the Supper, whenever it is served, should be a time of reorientation. It should be a time to return to basics—a time for quiet reflection and for honest evaluation of one's life in light of Calvary. The Supper is a time to humble ourselves before the Lord. It is a time for life adjustment, a time to repent, a time to worship. The Lord's Supper is also a time for us to recall what our Lord said just before He and the disciples sang a hymn and went out to the Mount of Olives: "I say to you, I will not drink of this fruit of the vine from now on until that day when I drink it new with you in My Father's kingdom" (Matt. 26:29).

What an encouragement it is to close the family gathering with those words of hope and anticipation—words that remind us of the day when the entire family, from every tribe and nation, will be gathered together for the first and final, never-ending time. This will be the *alpha* and *omega* meeting of God's whole family around the Lord's table in His Father's house! Meanwhile, we keep on remembering, we keep on proclaiming His death *until He returns! Hallelujah!*

Pastor, if the Lord's table is in disrepair in your church, do everything you can to repair it. Restore its meaning to the family, and reap the benefits of God's smile of approval. Only He knows, but one day the Lord may be pleased to meet your people in a life-changing encounter, as you and your family meet around His table. Remember, and live with that expectation.

Baptism: A Picture of Death and Resurrection

Could there be a more appropriate moment in the life of the church to worship the risen Christ than when a new believer is being baptized?

DEAR PASTOR,

A number of years ago while ministering in the Netherlands, Patricia and I were privileged to witness a baptismal service, one which had been planned for several months. Here, as in many parts of the world, the ordinance of baptism is given high priority in the life of the church. The practice is to wait until a certain number of candidates are ready, then devote an entire service to its observance. The importance of this event for these people cannot be overstated. When those who have made a profession of faith in Christ have gone through the required instruction on what it means to become a Christian and the responsibilities of church membership, they are put on the baptismal candidate list. As the time for baptism approaches, family members and friends are notified. Invitations to witness this special moment in their lives are both mailed and handed out.

That evening the church was packed with family, friends, and coworkers, many of whom did not know the Lord. Each candidate for baptism was introduced by the pastor and was asked questions relating to his or her faith and conversion. Then, after each had given testimony to what God had done and what this night meant to them, they were baptized. Each baptism was followed by a brief time of prayer and singing. When all had been baptized, the pastor summarized the meaning of what had taken place and extended an invitation to any who wished to put their faith in Christ. That evening several did, as God continued the process of adding to His church. Afterward, everyone joined in a celebration meal in the fellowship hall.

These believers considered baptism to be an important observance in the life of the church, as indeed it should be. The importance and sanctity of baptism were established by our Lord at the very beginning of His ministry: "Then Jesus came from Galilee to John at the Jordan to be baptized by him. And John tried to prevent Him, saying, 'I need to be baptized by You, and are You coming to me?' But Jesus answered and said to him, 'Permit it to be so now, for thus it is fitting for us to fulfill all righteousness.' Then he allowed Him. When He had been baptized, Jesus came up immediately from the water; and behold, the heavens were opened to Him, and He saw the Spirit of God descending like a dove and alighting upon Him. And suddenly a voice came from heaven, saying, 'This is My beloved Son, in whom I am well pleased'" (Matt. 3:13–17).

Jesus' actions publicly symbolized what would become the identifying act of public confession for all new converts. His baptism in the Jordan River can be seen as a picture of the day He would lay down His life, be buried, then triumph over death and the grave so that we, having been buried with Him, might also rise with Him to eternal life. In His baptism, Jesus was identifying with those He had come to save. Having been endorsed so clearly at the very inception of our Lord's ministry, it is easy to understand why, beginning at Pentecost, baptism became one of the requirements for entry into the Christian church.

You recall how Peter, on the Day of Pentecost, answered the question of the inquirers who asked what they should do to be saved. "Repent, and let every one of you be baptized in the name of Jesus Christ. . . .' Then those who gladly received his word were baptized; and that day about three thousand souls were added to them" (Acts 2:38, 41).

How more powerfully could the importance of baptism in the life of the believer and the church have been demonstrated? Just as we have seen that God's name is not simply a title but represents everything He is, so *baptism* is not just a word. Baptism illustrates our eternal identity with the greatest sacrifice ever made. We must never take it casually, for it places us in the tomb with our Savior where He was buried! It cries out in triumph, "He is risen, He is risen indeed." Baptism shouts to everyone who is watching, "Because He rose, I too have risen! Because He lives, I am alive! I am alive! The risen Christ resides in me! I am alive by His life. Hallelujah!"

> I have been made a new creation, with Christ I have been crucified;
> And what I was I am no longer, because I died when Jesus died!
>
> I have been made a new creation, though I was part of Adam's tree,
> I now am grafted into Jesus, I am in Him and He's in me!
>
> I can't explain, it is a mystery, I don't know how it can be true;
> I just accept what He's accomplished, I'm born again, all things are new![1]

That's it! That is what the one being baptized declares to those who are witnesses. The "old" has gone, the "new" has come! Sadly, however, this is not what happens in many of our churches today. How can it be when candidates, knowing little if anything about the faith they have embraced, are baptized with hardly a word of explanation other than their need to come that night a few minutes early, bring a towel, a change of clothes, and perhaps a hair dryer. Yet of even greater importance, how can the pastor be certain that the ones he is baptizing have really been born again, when he may not have talked to them more than five minutes before meeting them in the baptistry? I believe we assume people know more about what they are doing than we should. It is no longer a given that people in our part of the world understand the basics of Christianity, for there is little biblical orientation anymore.

I was reared in a tradition that required a waiting period before baptism, during which time instruction was given on the doctrine of salvation as well as what it meant to become a part of the Christian community, namely, the church. It was not enough for someone to "make a decision," for decisions could be insincere. The concern on the part of the church leaders was that Christ had committed Himself to me, not that I had "committed" myself to Him. They knew that decisions and commitments made by man often did not last any longer than a temporary feeling or emotion. Could this be why the majority of those making "decisions" today in the Western church cannot be found in church? In reality, they have never shown any evidence that God, the Holy Spirit, has taken up residence in their lives. There have been no visible changes, and they have little or no concern for the things of God. Yet they are church members. They have been baptized. They became one of us—or did they? Maybe they thought they had done all that was necessary to be guaranteed a flight to heaven by saying certain words, filling out a decision card, and being baptized.

Is a person's eligibility for baptism based on what he has done, or on what the Holy Spirit has done in Him? What if that person, in coming to the front at the close of a service, was simply responding to an emotion that had not yet touched the will? What if he had only been awakened to a spiritual need but did not yet really understand that being born again was in fact repenting, a turning around, to begin a brand-new life in Christ? How often the appeal today sounds more like an invitation to come and be rehabilitated rather than to come and die! More often than not, it does not even include a call to repentance. People are invited to come to Christ "if they have a problem," and He will "meet their need." A problem? Yes, we do have a problem, but it may not be what the person thinks it is. The problem of all humanity is that we have been born dead in sin and are headed toward a Christless eternity. There can be no new life without the death of the old. Are we giving those who express interest in the things of God a false sense of security? They walked the aisle; they registered a decision by signing a card; they said yes when asked the question; they made a commitment. But do these things in themselves mean that new birth has taken place?

I don't know why Pastor Moret of the Evangelical Church in Lausanne, Switzerland, made me wait longer than some others before I was baptized. I'm thankful that he did, though. I'm thankful that the church leaders loved me enough to make sure that, as far as they could tell, I had come to faith. A pastor friend once confided to me that if we were to make people in America wait several weeks or, as in my case, several months, most of them would not return to be baptized. He said they would lose interest! Lose interest? What is that saying? So we must baptize them as quickly as possible and put them on our rolls, with the realization that more than 50 percent of them aren't going to come back anyway. "But at least they have been baptized," we say. And *reported.* This may be one of the biggest sins in some of our American churches today.

Those who defend the position of immediate baptism cite examples in Scripture such as the day of Pentecost, the Ethiopian eunuch, and the Philippian jailer. In each of these examples, however, we must consider that there was an awesome fear of God and, as at Pentecost, a powerful conviction of sin that caused those who heard Peter's sermon to cry out, "What must we do to be saved?" If people in our services today were under such conviction of sin that they cried out, "Would someone please tell me how to be saved?" we would have a good argument for immediate baptism. But this is not what is happening.

Sometimes it seems as if, in some churches, baptism has become not much more than a hurdle to be negotiated on the way to church membership. What impact is this holy ordinance having on the "unbeliever" sitting in the pew, when so little time and importance are given to such an awesome picture of redemption? What is it saying to our children about the importance of baptism when we baptize at the beginning of a service, before everyone has even settled down and stopped talking?

Even if what I am saying were an exception to the rule, it would still be a concern. Tragically, however, it is the norm in many of our churches. Baptism no longer holds the place of importance it should. Henry and Marilynn Blackaby told me of an experience they had in one of the large churches of our land, where people were being baptized while the offering was being taken and the choir was singing. That part of the service was like a "three-ring church"!

How can this happen? It happens because when something has lost its significance, it can be squeezed in anywhere. And in today's church, there is so much to squeeze in. How often baptism is "stuck on" to the beginning of a service, and, more often than not, no other reference will be made to it. While the baptized are getting "dried and dressed," the service continues with not much more than a passing, "Let's hear a hearty 'Amen.'" Does not such a significant moment in the life of the believer and church deserve more careful attention?

Several years ago in a Midwest church, Patricia and I were sitting in the front row ten minutes or so before the service was to begin. We had been advised by the pastor that he was going to begin with baptism. We noticed a lady distributing sheets of paper to those who had already assembled. When she got to us, she explained that she was one of those who was going to be baptized. She went on to explain that she had asked if she could give her testimony before being immersed, but had been told that there would not be enough time. In any case, this was not usually done. Wanting so badly to let the "witnesses" know what God had done in her life, she had typed up her testimony that afternoon and was now handing it out. We talked with her for a moment and discovered that she had recently moved to the United States from another country. In her native land, professing Christ publicly often cost the convert dearly. Consequently, public baptism was a very significant moment in the life of the candidate and the church. We read her testimony of how God in His mercy had led her to the United States, where she had met Him. What a powerful witnessing opportunity was missed that night—because there wasn't enough time.

Pastor, do the waters of baptism hold the significance they should in the minds of your people? Have they become just a pool through which someone who has filled out a card has to pass on the way to full membership? Do the candidates you baptize understand the profound implications this observance has for their lives? Do you give enough time for the true meaning of what is taking place to be really understood by each candidate? Do you need to consider spending more time counseling with the new believer, making sure that new birth has actually taken place? Church staff, do you need to allow extra time for the candidates to bear witness to their newfound faith? Do you give a clear closing word about the meaning of baptism to those who have been watching?

The weight of importance given to baptism by our Lord is again demonstrated in His final recorded word to His disciples in Matthew 28:18–20. He gives them a command and places it right between the discipling and teaching of all nations. "And Jesus came and spoke to them, saying, 'All authority has been given to Me in heaven and on earth. Go therefore and make disciples of all the nations, b*aptizing them* in the name of the Father and of the Son and of the Holy Spirit, teaching them to observe all things that I have commanded you; and lo, I am with you always, even to the end of the age.'"

Could there be a more appropriate moment in the life of the church to worship the risen Christ, to ritualize His victory over death and the grave, to bow before the Savior in humble adoration, to thank Him for His incomparable gift, than when a new believer is being baptized? What a moment to rejoice, when one who has been given every opportunity to understand what salvation really is, and has given evidence that he has passed from death to life, goes through the waters. And if there ever was an opportunity to present the claims of Christ, it is at that moment when that picture, painted by our

Lord in the Jordan River, is again portrayed to another group of witnesses. But how often we miss it.

The Puritan John Owen beautifully capsulized in these nine words what baptism truly symbolizes: "the death of death in the death of Christ." May the sanctity and meaning of that which is so often made common be restored to our churches today. May the careful handling of this ordinance bring our people to a deeper sense of reverence and awe at what God has done for us in Christ. And every time the baptismal waters are stirred, may this be a time of celebration, thanksgiving, and *worship*.

The Call of the Director of Music

The Levites who were the singers . . . stood at the east end of the altar,
clothed in white linen . . . when the trumpeters and singers were as one,
to make one sound to be heard in praising and thanking the LORD,
and when they lifted up their voice with the trumpets and cymbals and
instruments of music, and praised the LORD, saying: "For He is good,
For His mercy endures forever," that the house, the house of the LORD,
was filled with a cloud . . . for the glory of the LORD filled the house of God.
—2 Chronicles 5:12–14

DEAR MINISTER OF MUSIC,

You may recall that I pointed out in an earlier letter that you don't have to have music to worship and that many today mistakenly think of the music portion of the service as "the worship time." Though this may be true, it goes without saying that music *is* one of God's greatest gifts to His children to use in expressing to Him their love, adoration, thanksgiving, and praise, along with the host of other things such as confession, commitment, and surrender.

If it is worship time when God's people have gathered, it is a time for music. It is a time to sing to God and to each other in psalms, hymns, and spiritual songs, just as the apostle Paul admonished the church in Colossae to do: "Let the word of Christ dwell in you richly in all wisdom, teaching and admonishing one another in psalms and hymns and spiritual songs, singing with grace in your hearts to the Lord" (Col. 3:16).

It is not coincidental that the singing of psalms, hymns, and spiritual songs is linked with having the word of Christ dwelling in the singer richly in wisdom. "Dwell in you richly" actually means to "fill the house with riches." This Scripture forcefully speaks of our being filled with the riches of God's Word, out of which will issue true worship.

Paul gives almost the same instruction to the church in Ephesus, only this time he connects the singing and the singer to being filled with the Spirit. "Do not be drunk with wine, in which is dissipation; but be filled with the Spirit, speaking to one another in psalms and hymns and spiritual songs, singing and making melody in your heart to the Lord, giving thanks always for all things to God the Father in the name of our Lord Jesus Christ" (Eph. 5:18–20).

To "be filled with the Spirit" was not a suggestion Paul was making; it was a command. *"Be filled"* actually means "be continuously being filled." God's setting of such a high standard for music's role in the life of the church underscores its importance. It is obvious that it should never simply be "music for music's sake." If it is to meet God's requirements, the music we play and sing must issue out of the riches of God's Word and the fullness of His Spirit in us. This is fundamental to everything we do in music ministry. One who has no desire for the riches of God in his or her life, whether the most outstanding singer or musician you have ever heard, or whether sitting in the pew on a Sunday morning, has nothing to offer God, either in service or worship, that is acceptable to Him. This is our beginning point.

This high standard for music leadership was established in the Old Testament. In 1 Chronicles 15:2, we read that the Levites (the musicians) were the ones chosen of God to carry the ark. "No one may carry the ark of God but the Levites, for the LORD has chosen them to carry the ark of God and to minister before Him forever."

The Levites were appointed to special tasks in service of the Lord. In chapters 15–16 of 1 Chronicles, we see that Asaph and his brethren were appointed to minister before the ark continually, while others were appointed to give thanks unto the Lord. In 2 Chronicles 5:12–14 and in Nehemiah 12:27–29 we read of "singers" being appointed to ministry. But not only were the musicians chosen and appointed; they were "set apart" for their ministry. Numbers 8:5–14 depicts the entire ceremony which prepared the ministers and leaders for service. In verse 6, we hear God's order through Moses to "take the Levites from among the children of Israel and cleanse them."

In 2 Chronicles 5:11–14, we have the moving account of the priests withdrawing from the holy place where the ark had been placed. They were never again to return, for from that point on only the high priest would be allowed to enter the holy of holies once a year, on the Day of Atonement. As they withdrew, all the musicians stood on the east side of the altar, dressed in white linen. Some of them had cymbals, some had stringed instruments, and others had harps. There were trumpeters and singers, and when they all came together "as one" in their praising of God for His goodness, "the glory of the LORD filled the house of God" (v. 14). What a sight and sound that must have been! How exciting to think that right in the middle of it all were the musicians who had been chosen by God, set apart and assigned to their respective duties, singing and playing to the Lord. And they were dressed in white linen—a symbol of purity.

God's standard for His musicians has not changed. It carries over to the New Testament and into our day. It is not just a job for someone who is musically talented. Musicians who are truly serving the Lord will have "His Word dwelling in them." The first requirement is that they will "be filled with the Holy Spirit." They will exhibit the fruit of the Spirit as found in Galatians 5. They will not use the excuse of being a "temperamental musician" when their temper, ego, or impatience gets the upper hand because they will recognize these as sin from which they need to repent.

Fellow Musician, the importance of the calling God has placed on your life should not be underestimated. It is one of the major influences in the life of the church as a whole and in the life of His people individually. I have always been fascinated by how many of the psalms were written specifically "for the director of music." They were given to him to arrange for voices and instruments, to prepare and rehearse, and to teach the congregation. The vehicle we have been given to use is, in itself, one of the most powerful tools ever put into the hands of man.

When music is used under the influence of the Holy Spirit, it not only prepares the way for the Lord to speak, but it is also what God uses to reach deep into the hearts of men and women in a way that nothing else seems capable of doing. It can soften hearts that have become hardened and resistant toward Him. It can comfort anxious souls, calm distressed spirits, and turn despair into hope. It can carry people to heights of celebration and adoration otherwise unattainable. It is one of God's most glorious gifts, and He has placed it in your hands, Director of Music, to use for His glory and for the edification of His people.

But just as music has the potential for being a highway over which God can travel in great blessing, it has equal potential of being an obstacle that can get in His way. We ought not to be surprised that anything with such power would be used by the enemy, since he knows it can be as great a force for evil as it is for good. I believe that music, under the control of the flesh, can cause more damage in the life of the church and do more to undermine what God wants to do than almost anything else.

As the director of music, your assignment is multifaceted. You must select music, rehearse choirs and ensembles, lead worship services, and a host of other things. In addition to these basic responsibilities, there is a dimension to your calling that is often overlooked, yet I'm convinced it is fundamental to everything you do. Without attention to this, no matter how excellent or successful your "program" may be, chances are it will be a failure in God's eyes. I am speaking about your responsibility to lead those who work with you to a basic understanding of what true ministry is, what true worship is, and what their calling and assignment is as worship facilitators.

Singers and musicians who do not understand what God's requirements are for them can end up doing more harm than good. Church musicians who see themselves only as performers of religious music are no better than a pastor who sees himself strictly as a public speaker. He may deliver a polished speech, but it is devoid of anything spiritual. Performers may impress people with their abilities; they may attract a following; they may receive the applause of the crowds; they may enjoy what they are doing. But if they do not understand their fundamental assignment, they will not fulfill God's calling for their lives, and while attracting attention to themselves, they are detracting attention from God.

Because of the very nature of music, there is inherent in the call to music ministry the potential of being man-centered rather than God-centered. Because of its nature and the temperaments that often accompany those gifted in this area, it can easily become the womb for growing egos, the breeding ground for competitiveness and jealousy, and the incubator of major conflict within the church. I have heard the music ministry of a church referred to as the "war department." Someone has said that when Lucifer was cast out of heaven, he landed in the choir loft. Though we may chuckle at this, we really should be grieved at how often it is true.

In some places, the music department has become a world unto itself. I've observed church music ministries that have become so important that the rest of the church's ministries seem to have to revolve around them. To our shame, in many churches choir rehearsals are held during prayer meeting time, giving the impression that singing or playing is more important than praying. Because of this, there are churches God has actually visited in revival and has been able to touch every area of the church except the music.

Because of the very nature of the medium, there is the potential of operating more in the flesh than in the Spirit. As I have said before, it is often among us singers and musicians that *God is "used" to display man's talent, rather than man's talent used to display God.* When this happens, our music amounts to nothing more than sounding brass and tinkling symbols in God's sight. Any offering which is not acceptable to God will bring no spiritual or eternal benefit to the people, no matter how much they may enjoy what they hear and do. We may succeed in leading them to an emotional high. We may even bring the preacher out of his chair and the people out of their pews; but if we haven't led them to God, we have failed in our calling. If what we have done has attracted the people more to ourselves than to God, we have failed in our mission. *We are not called to be entertainers of the people; we are called to be ministers of the gospel.* May the standard God has set for us be the standard for which we all strive.

The Language and Power of Music

*The fundamental question in determining whether something is right or wrong is not,
What are the consequences? or, Does it fit into the way people think? or even,
Will the result be favorable or unfavorable? The fundamental question must be,
Does it adhere to the standards of God as set forth in His Word?*

DEAR DIRECTOR OF MUSIC,

In my last letter to you, I referred to the power that is inherent in music.
Many today insist that music is amoral, that there is nothing innately good or bad
about music itself. They say it is neutral, and only its use determines whether it is
good or evil. To a degree this is true, but in a very real way music ceases to be
neutral the moment those little black-and-white notes begin to be woven together
to produce certain combinations of sounds that result in the message or worldview that the composer of the music wants to get across. The music itself
becomes a statement, even when words are not attached to its message.

By the testimony of the composers and musicians themselves, a large portion of the secular music of the last forty years has been birthed in rebellion—
rebellion against the authority of state, church, and family. It was, and often
still is, an attempt to overturn anything that represents tradition. In a real
sense, it is a thumbing of the nose at the Judeo-Christian principles upon
which our Western world's society has been based. It has been an effort—and
a very successful one—to throw things out of balance. Millions have been
marching to its drumbeat. This music has not only become a vehicle for entertainment; it has become a spiritual force in people's lives. To many it has
become a religion, and it is as real to them as traditional religion is to others.

The Scottish poet Carlyle is purported to have once said: "Let me make a nation's music, and I care not who makes her laws. I will control that nation." To a significant degree this has been true for our country. What started out as a mild reaction by a new generation to society's status quo soon became a way of life that led to, and was nurtured by, drugs. For many years the two went hand in hand. The music, both written and recorded, expressed in no uncertain terms the mind-set and developing worldview of those espousing this rebellion and lifestyle. You did not have to hear the words to know what the music was saying. Its message rang loud and clear. It captured more and more hearts as it became the god before which a large part of the populace was bowing and worshiping. Music became god, and any challenge to this god was, and still is, met with a closed mind. It is an unnegotiable area and will be defended "to the death." It is very personal. Any subject is open for discussion except "my music."

Before going any further, I need to clarify that I am not saying that nothing of real value has been written over these last decades. This would be far from the truth. Some of the most beautiful music and lyrics have been composed during these years. I am not in the camp that holds to the philosophy that if music doesn't have a 1940s or earlier sound it is not acceptable. I am not one who rejects a syncopated beat or who believes that guitars and drums have no place in the life of the church. I do believe, however, that as Christians we must be discerning. We must judge all things and never be guilty of an "anything goes" attitude toward music. Just because people like it certainly does not mean it is right. Actually, if it is a sound that a rebellious world endorses, this in itself should raise a caution flag.

Every generation has had its music. I recall when Patricia and I were beginning in ministry (when we were young!), a good bit of the music we were doing was on the cutting edge. Some of the songs had more "beat" than some fellow Christians liked. We actually upset some traditionalists. But the music we did was never out of balance. The music was saying what the words were saying. There was an honest marriage between the message and the music. The melodies and harmonies never were overcome by the beat. The rhythm supported the overall thrust of the song and never became the driving force. If anything was a driving force in those days, it probably was the words. But combined with music that was speaking the same language, it became a powerful medium. The songs actually would have "made it" without the beat, whereas today, I wonder how many of the songs would actually be performed or listened to were it not for the driving, loud rhythm. Until recent years there has always seemed to be a healthy balance between the melody, harmony, and rhythm.

Dear Director of Music, let me restate what I said at the beginning of my last letter to you. You have in your hands one of the most powerful tools God has ever given mankind. This has been recognized by the secular world, as well as by God's people, for thousands of years. In his *Politics*, Aristotle made the following statement: "Music directly imitates [represents] the passions of the soul, hence when one listens to ignoble music that imitates a certain passion he becomes imbued with the same passion; and if over a long time he habitually listens to the kind of music that arouses ignoble passions, his whole character will be shaped to an ignoble form. In short, if one listens to the wrong kind of music he will become the wrong kind of person."

We are obviously not the first generation to ponder the incredible power of music in the lives of people. More attention is currently being given to the effects of music on the human personality than perhaps in all of history. Music touches every level of our lives. My wife Patricia has done research in this area, and though there is not time in this letter to get into all these levels, let me just touch on several things that she has found in her study. One is that music has major physiological effects on people. Clinical researchers at the Georgia Baptist Medical Center in Atlanta discovered that premature or low-weight babies gained weight faster and used oxygen more efficiently when they listened to music. Babies exposed to one and one-half hours of music each day averaged only eleven days in the intensive care unit, compared with sixteen days for those who did not listen to music.

After classical music was provided in critical care units at Baltimore's Saint Agnus Hospital, the need for medicine to control pain or anxiety decreased dramatically. One doctor said that half an hour of music produced the same effect as ten milligrams of Valium.

Music also has a significant effect on the brain and children's ability to learn. The February 19, 1996, issue of *Newsweek* carried an article entitled "Why Do Schools Flunk Biology?" that addresses the positive power of music in education. In it, Lynnell Hancock writes: "Plato once said that music 'is a more potent instrument than any other for education.' Now scientists know why. Music, they believe, trains the brain for higher forms of thinking. Researchers at the University of California, Irvine, studied the power of music by observing two groups of preschoolers. One group took piano lessons and sang daily in chorus. The other did not. After eight months the musical three-year-olds were expert puzzle masters, scoring 80 percent higher than their playmates did in spatial intelligence—the ability to visualize the world accurately. 'Early music training can enhance a child's ability to reason,' says Irvine physicist Gordon Shaw. 'Yet music education is often the first "frill" to be cut when school budgets shrink.'"

Director of Music, Children's Choir Director, have you realized that even as you are teaching children about God through the songs they are learning, you are contributing to their ability to learn and reason? Isn't that one of the reasons God has given us music?

Another area of our lives music touches in a powerful way is in the area of our *emotions*. The realm of the emotions is probably the most influential one when it comes to the matter of styles and tastes. Everyone has acquired tastes for certain styles. If you were to ask someone, "Why do you want to listen to that kind of music?" many times the answer would be, "I like the way it makes me feel." Music has immense power over our emotions. I address this more completely in my letter to you on "Adrenaline Highs Versus the Holy Spirit."

Many scientific studies have also been made relating to the *behavioral* effects music has on people, but the best place to look at this is in Scripture. Here we find the uniqueness of music and its power on behavior, particularly in the spiritual realm exemplified for us. In 1 Samuel 16:14–18, 23, we read the story of Saul being troubled by an evil spirit. You will recall that his counselors recommended he call for someone to play on the harp, since they knew of the positive effects it would have on him. David, who at that time was still tending his father's sheep, was summoned. "And so it was, whenever the spirit from God was upon Saul, that David would take a harp and play it with his hand. Then Saul would become refreshed and well, and the distressing spirit would depart from him" (v. 23).

Looking back to the thirteenth verse of this chapter, we find that David was one upon whom the Holy Spirit rested. Not only did his skillful playing help the situation, but there was something about the music David selected and played that had an expulsive power over the forces of evil. There is a vast difference between one who is simply a talented, skillful musician and one who is enabled and guided by the Holy Spirit. Music, in itself a powerful tool, becomes increasingly so when used in the hands of an anointed servant of God.

There are other instances in Scripture that give us glimpses into the powerful spiritual influence music can have. On many occasions music was used by prophets to accompany their prophesying. First Chronicles 25:1 tells about David and the commanders of the army setting apart some of the sons of Asaph, Heman, and Jeduthun, "who should prophesy with harps, stringed instruments, and cymbals."

Let me stress again my conviction that music itself is a language. It does not have to have words to convey a message. We must be especially spiritually alert when it comes to discerning whether the music or arrangement of a song carries the same message as the text. I believe I can best illustrate what I am saying by sharing an experience I had some years ago.

Several "hard rock" radio stations in Brussels, Belgium, asked me to host a weekly, two-hour program of "Christian" rock music. These stations knew there was music in the Christian world that matched "their sound" and felt that there was a potential listening audience that would tune in to hear new songs not readily available in the stores. They wanted the program to be hosted in English for the growing English-speaking population of this NATO capital. There were no restrictions as to what I could say, who I could interview, the witness I could share, or the literature I could offer, as long as I remained faithful to the station's "sound." The International Baptist Church of Brussels, through whom the invitation had been initially extended, offered to undergird the effort in prayer as well as provide a phone counselor during the times the programs were being aired.

After several months of programming, the stations notified me that the music was not "hard" enough. They had no quarrel with my having aired interviews with Christian athletes, read Scripture, talked about the Lord, and offered free literature to the listeners. Their problem was with the sound. They were right in saying that I had not "gone as far" as their sound was, though there was ample Christian rock available with that sound. After wading through hundreds of solo and group albums, however, my wife and I had come to the conviction that there was a point beyond which I could not go. I had already gone well beyond my personal tastes. After seeking counsel and prayer, I knew I could not continue.

Now before some of you chastise me for being a prude and forfeiting the opportunity to share the gospel on these secular stations, let me tell you what I learned from two Belgian Christians who had been doing essentially the same kind of thing, but in the French language. Having decided I could not go on, I went to these two to ask them what kind of response they had received in their over two years in operation. I knew they had been very clear in their presentation of the gospel. They also had someone manning a phone while the programs were being aired and had been offering Bibles and literature. Saturating each program, however, was hard, metallic "Christian" rock. What they told me was a complete surprise. In those two years they had been contacted by only one person who phoned in for a Bible. I realize that the Lord may very well have been speaking to people who did not call in for help, but one contact in two years? How could that be?

I gave it much thought and concluded that the powerful message of the music might be canceling out the message of the words. What other explanation could there be? Their program had one of the larger listening audiences. The listeners, however, were seemingly untouched by the gospel, while loving the music. And this was music that had a Christian message.

Music *is* a language! When choosing music for use in the church, we must be careful not to choose music that cancels out the message of the words. One of the most needful gifts in the church today is the gift of discernment. In his letter to the church in Philippi, the apostle Paul said: "This is my prayer: that your love may abound more and more in knowledge and depth of insight, so that you may be able to discern what is best and may be pure and blameless until the day of Christ" (Phil. 1:9–10 NIV). The Amplified Version reads, "That you may surely learn to sense what is vital . . . recognizing the highest and the best, and distinguishing the moral differences."

Many times we make musical choices based on what we like or don't like. Yet we know as Christians that in other areas of life, there are plenty of things we don't do that we might like because we have learned from Scripture that those "likes" don't align with God's standards. We have learned to take into account the truth of our fallen humanity and sin's effect on us. We know that "good old human nature" may be old, but it is certainly not good, and we cannot afford to do just as we like.

What about those things that are not spelled out so clearly in Scripture? In this verse from Philippians it is presupposed for those who will be discerning that their love for God and for one another is abounding more and more "in knowledge and depth of insight." In the next chapter of this letter to the church at Philippi, Paul talked about having the mind of Christ operative in us. In other passages of Scripture, we are admonished to abide in Christ and to let His Word abide in us. This is fundamental to living the Christian life in the fullness that God has provided and to making the choices and decisions that will please Him. It is especially true if we are going to choose the music that most glorifies Him—music that best interprets who He is.

Adrenaline Highs or the Holy Spirit?

Right thinking is fundamental to offering God acceptable worship.
Some people turn their minds off when they sing in church.
Though the apostle Paul does talk about praying in the spirit as well as with
the understanding, we must be careful not to equate an empty head
with being in the Spirit. Worship or celebration with an empty head
will result in an empty offering.

DEAR DIRECTOR OF MUSIC,

Several years ago, I was given a book written by a Christian psychiatrist that was a thorough examination of the effects of adrenaline on man's behavior. Though I have since misplaced the book, I remember reading with fascination how research showed that adrenaline addiction can produce symptoms as real as those resulting from some drugs. I could personally relate to what the research had shown, because I was addicted to adrenaline.

At that stage in my life I was a runner. My exercise had evolved beyond jogging for health reasons. I ran a minimum of forty miles a week. My running "habit" had become so important and necessary to me that nearly everything else revolved around it. It was the one thing that I could not, or would not, do without. I had all the symptoms of someone who could not function normally without getting my "high." Though I was deeply involved in ministry, running was more important to me than my quiet time with the Lord. When I went to bed at night, I couldn't wait to get up early the next morning to run. If I didn't get to run two mornings in a row, I would begin to feel depressed. I suppose you could say I was experiencing withdrawal from my "runner's high," which could rightly be called an "adrenaline high."

The research also showed that music can have a profound impact on the human body, especially on its level of adrenaline. This is an area that should cause us great concern. It seems that many in church music leadership are unaware of the powerful effects music can have on people, especially on their emotions. In my last letter to you I expressed my conviction that music in itself is a language that speaks strongly to man's soul. Though many may never have considered it, this is not a new concept. Even in the 1600s, composer Claudio Monteverdi asserted that the end of all music is to affect the soul. Music affects the soul because it is an expression of man's soul. As such it speaks forcefully to the emotions, since the soul is the seat of the emotions. A person's emotions can be driven by music, resulting in a multitude of physical manifestations.

I watched this happen several months ago in a national conference for a specific group of evangelistic leaders. One evening a choir from a neighboring city led in a period of "worship." At one point the leader taught a simple, catchy, rhythmic chorus: *"Lord, we want to see You."* After singing it several times, I began to count. We sang this same phrase over and over, sometimes punctuated with a comment or Scripture. From the time I started counting, we repeated this chorus *eighteen times,* with numerous modulations. By the time we had finished, nearly everyone was on his feet, having been worked up to quite an emotional high. This group, by the way, would be considered conservative. The continuous repetition of words and melody, accompanied by the incessant beat, effectively led a group of normally serious-minded men to an adrenaline high.

This type of constant repetition, which has become common in our churches, can be extremely dangerous. Not only can it produce an addictive "adrenaline high," but it can also actually lead to an altered state of consciousness that disengages the mind and leaves a person highly suggestible. In his book *Counterfeit Revival* author and speaker Hank Hanegraaff discussed this in great detail, using powerful examples to expose the dangers inherent in this type of repetition.[1] Those who desire to control others or lead them into error are well aware of its power and seem to be able to use it quite effectively to accomplish their own ends.

How often have you heard or sung something like "Lord, we want to see You" over and over until the words and music have almost hypnotized those who are singing? If the music is rhythmic enough, an entire congregation can reach an emotional "praise" high. The questions we must ask are: "What is this accomplishing? Is telling the Lord over and over again that we want to see Him going to make Him more inclined to reveal Himself to us?"

In His Sermon on the Mount, Jesus gave us these instructions: "And when you pray, do not use vain repetitions as the heathen do. For they think that they will be heard for their many words. Therefore do not be like them" (Matt. 6:7–8). When we participate in this type of repetitive, mantra-like chanting, are we guilty of doing as the heathen do? Do we really hope that somehow we will get God's attention by repeating the same thing over and over, or are we in fact doing it for the high it gives us?

Director of Music, be careful how you play with the emotions of the people God has entrusted to your leadership and care. Be careful that your people do not become so accustomed to getting a "praise high" when they come to church that a service seems empty if they do not experience it. Many today hop from group to group, from church to church, looking for higher highs. The tragedy is that they have been led to believe that what they are experiencing is the Holy Spirit, when it is nothing more than an intense emotional response.

I pray that this letter will serve as a reminder to you, as it has been to me, of how critical it is to guard the balance between the soul and the spirit. We must constantly be aware of the power inherent in this marvelous gift God has given us to use—the gift of music. We must be discerning. We must ever keep before us what our Lord said to the Samaritan woman at Jacob's well: "God is Spirit, and those who worship Him must worship in spirit and truth" (John 4:24).

Discerning between the Holy and the Common

Therefore, since we are receiving a kingdom which cannot be shaken, let us have grace, by which we may serve God acceptably with reverence and godly fear. For our God is a consuming fire.
—Hebrews 12:28

DEAR DIRECTOR OF MUSIC,

In the past several years there has been a disturbing trend in the North American church, and it seems to be growing. Many churches are increasingly allowing, and even inviting, unbelievers to participate in their choirs or orchestras. As a result, I hear this question being asked with increasing frequency: "Should we be involving unbelievers in areas of worship leadership in our churches?" This is a serious question, and it deserves serious consideration. In order to give an adequate answer, we need to understand why this is happening and what God would have to say about it.

As I have already pointed out in several other letters to you, there has been a major shift in recent years in the way we view worship in the church. Whereas God and His desires were once the primary focus of all that happened in our services, now mankind and his desires are often seen as central. Many worship leaders now seem to be motivated and controlled by a kind of fear—not an appropriate fear of God, but fear of the people not "enjoying themselves." What many of them don't realize, however, is that when the likes and dislikes of the people are put first, we are stealing from God what is primarily His, and we are profaning that which God intended to be holy and wholly His.

In our zeal to minister to needs, to reach the world with the gospel, we have convinced ourselves that people are our top priority. The motto of the western evangelical church today might very well be, "People matter most." Although this may sound good on the surface, in reality it is contrary to what Scripture says. We have reversed God's order, and rather than our service coming out of our worship—worship concentrated solely on God—we view worship as a tool. We see it as a means to an end, not as something important enough to spend time in it alone.

Scripture gives us a vivid example of one who exhibited the attitude that "people matter most"—Judas. Remember how incensed he was at the waste of the precious ointment poured on Jesus' feet? This ointment might have been sold for much, and the money given to the poor. But Jesus did not consider the ointment poured on His feet as a waste, any more than He considered the time Mary spent sitting at His feet when a meal needed to be prepared as wasted time. In fact, He commended Mary for choosing the better part.

We are so disoriented to the ways of God today that we have difficulty accepting the fact that God should have priority over man's needs. We have convinced ourselves that the only proper gift to God is one that benefits people. Perhaps an apt description of the church today would be: "The church lives for others first, then the church lives for God."

Worship Leader, the fundamental question we need to be asking ourselves is not, "Is what we are doing pleasing to the people?" but, "Is what we are doing pleasing to God?" The church is called to be first and foremost "Christ serving." Our worship today often expresses more love for people than for God, which has resulted in a more person-conscious approach than a God-conscious one. Worship that is man-centered is untrue to the very nature of the God we say we've come to worship. When the value we place on what we do in worship lies in the effect it has on the worshiper rather than the effect it has on God, we are prostituting the very thing God has given us to meet Him. This is one area in which the holy becomes common.

True worship must always reflect God's nature while expressing the adoration of the worshiper. Charles Wesley expressed it accurately when he wrote: "The holy to the holy leads." But when our concentration is on our own feelings and needs, we turn away from the Holy One and focus on the common. According to our Lord Jesus, the first and greatest commandment is "Love the

LORD your God with all your heart, with all your soul, and with all your mind." The second was like it: "Love your neighbor as yourself" (Matt. 22:37, 39). We have reversed the order.

The tendency to focus on the desires of people and neglect the desires of God is not new. In Ezekiel 44:10–23, we read about the distinction between the sons of Zadok, who were to minister to God, and the sons of Levi, who were to minister to the people. In this passage God makes abundantly clear that it is a higher vocation to stand before Him to minister to Him than it is to stand before the people to minister to them.

This in no way implies that people are not important or that their needs should not be met. People do matter. Anyone who knows anything of Calvary will never try to use God's being more important as an excuse not to care for people. Jesus made this clear when He criticized the Pharisees and scribes for having this attitude toward their parents (Mark 7:11). People do matter, but they do not matter more than God. The people in this passage in Ezekiel were not to be neglected. Far from it, for they were to be taught the difference between the holy and common, the clean and unclean. But it was the Levite sons of Zadok who were to teach them. Because the other Levites had gone along with how the people wanted to worship, they had been demoted to taking charge of the gates, slaughtering the burnt offerings, and standing before the people to serve them. As a consequence of having turned the holy into the profane in worship, God said of these sons of Levi: "They shall not come near Me to minister to Me as priest, nor come near any of My holy things, nor into the Most Holy Place" (Ezek. 44:13).

On the other hand, the sons of Zadok who had "faithfully carried out the duties of my sanctuary when the Israelites went astray from me, are to come near to minister before me; they are to stand before me to offer sacrifices. . . . They alone are to enter my sanctuary; they alone are to come near my table to minister before me and perform my service" (vv. 15–16 NIV). All of these blessings came as a result of refusing to go along with the people in the way they wanted to worship! The sons of Zadok refused to desecrate or make common the worship that was God's alone. It is an awesome thing to worship a holy God. It is even more awesome to be called to be worship leaders.

This brings us to our fundamental question: What about involving unbelievers in the music ministry of the church? The tendency to do so is done in hopes that bringing the unredeemed under the preaching of the gospel in this

150

way will lead them to faith. I understand this line of thinking, and I also understand that quite often the abilities of these gifted people add significantly to the quality of the music. But I also see this as a sign of the lowering of God's standards for worship. It is again saying that people matter most. We seem to be forgetting that *choir members and instrumentalists are worship leaders!* When we invite "the world" to participate in leading worship, we are making common that which God calls holy.

What do you think God would say about allowing the unredeemed to participate in leading the sacrifices of praise and adoration to Him? The fact is, He already has said something about this. All we have to do is go back a few verses in Ezekiel to hear Him saying: "'When you brought in foreigners, uncircumcised in heart and uncircumstanced in flesh, to be in My sanctuary to defile it—My house—and when you offered My food, the fat and the blood, then they broke My covenant because of all your abominations. And you have not kept charge of My holy things, but you have set others to keep charge of My sanctuary for you.' Thus says the Lord GOD: 'No foreigner, uncircumcised in heart or uncircumcised in flesh, shall enter My sanctuary, including any foreigner who is among the children of Israel'" (Ezek. 44:7–9).

I believe this speaks for itself. The Levites were demoted to serving the people because they had defiled the sanctuary by allowing nonbelievers to participate in the offerings. When we allow unbelievers to assume the responsibilities of worship leadership, are we not doing the same thing? Are we not treating the holy things of God as though they were common?

Standing before God to lead His people in worship is an awesome privilege and responsibility, regardless of the area of leadership. We must not knowingly allow anything to hinder what we do. In the twelfth chapter of Hebrews, the writer admonished us to throw off everything that could encumber us and run with perseverance the race set before us, keeping our eyes fixed on Jesus. He went on to talk about God's discipline and spoke of the holy life we are called to live. He talked about the awe and reverence Moses had for God, and he spoke about the New Covenant in which we now have a mediator, the God-Man, Jesus Christ. He summed up the roll call of faith and the call to holiness with these words: "Therefore . . . let us be thankful, and so worship God acceptably with reverence and awe, for our God is a consuming fire" (vv. 28–29 NIV).

In light of the holiness of God; in light of our being children of God; in light of our receiving a kingdom that cannot be shaken; in light of the shed blood of Jesus Christ; in light of the fact that "once more I will shake not only the earth but also the heavens" (Heb. 12:26 NIV), when we worship we must do so with reverence and awe, for our God is a holy God. He is a consuming fire. Let us not become guilty of turning the holy into the common.

To Applaud or Not to Applaud?

The Response Factor in Worship

Give unto the LORD, O you mighty ones,
Give unto the LORD glory and strength.
Give unto the LORD the glory due to His name;
Worship the LORD in the beauty of holiness.
—Psalm 29:1–2

DEAR WORSHIP LEADER,

I am often asked the question, "Do you think we should applaud in church?" This has become another of those controversial areas where a simple yes or no answer is not enough. The real issue goes much deeper than whether it is ever appropriate to clap our hands in a worship service. Should we applaud or not? is not the question we should be asking ourselves. Instead, we need to be asking, "What is the most God-honoring way to *respond* in the context of worship?" To *respond* is right; to *respond correctly* is of utmost importance.

I am writing this letter to you because it is our responsibility as worship leaders not only to help the people encounter God in worship but also to assist them in making appropriate responses—responses that keep the focus on the One we are worshiping and not turn the focus toward people. The problem has been that little thought seems to have been given to this, and worship leaders have gone along with whatever responses their congregations have made, when very often these responses have been "in the flesh" and not "in the Spirit."

Today we go from one extreme to the other. We have churches that make no visible or audible response at all, while others applaud everything. I hope this letter will help bring the two closer together. I believe, under the guidance of the Holy Spirit, it is your responsibility to guide the people in making the appropriate response. We all know that the Lord is primarily looking for the response of the heart. It doesn't matter what we do outwardly if our hearts are not right, for the Lord will not accept what we offer. This does not mean, however, that an outward, physical expression is not legitimate. We are, after all, physical and emotional beings.

Because there has been so little instruction in this area, what is often done is purely in the flesh for the flesh. A little counsel, however, can go a long way toward helping your people know what to do.

In some traditions, the only time allowed for any outward response is at the end of the service. That is when the "response" or "invitation" hymn is sung. That is when the "appeal" is made, so everyone waits until that part of the service to do anything. By then, however, something may have happened that needed an immediate response, but the program went on without any time for reflection, and the impact of that moment was forgotten.

Then there are those traditions in which encouraging people to make any kind of public response is considered unnecessary coaching and a usurping of the role of the Holy Spirit. I believe that this is a legitimate concern, for in some circles there is a tendency to manipulate people's emotions, resulting in decisions made that effect no change in the decider's life. An emotional response that does not *engage the will* does not have any eternal value. Yet, I say again, *response is central to worship.*

Every worship encounter recorded in Scripture resulted in a response of the worshiper. Not to respond is not to worship. Those who say they have worshiped but have not made any response to God do not understand what worship is. The very act of worship is a response to the object of our worship. Christian worship is a response to the God who is there, to the God who "so loved." There may be times in your life, as there have been in mine, when the emotions run dry and the "feelings" are absent, yet you respond in faith to who you know God to be. Worship is as much an engagement of the will as it is a stirring of the emotions. We worship God for who He is, not because we feel like it. Worship Leader, I do not believe that we are engaged in true worship when emotions only are involved. I do believe, however, that you can have true worship—that which God accepts—when the will alone is engaged. We may not feel like it, but we can *choose* to worship.

I can't help but think of the many times I've heard Dr. Stephen Olford tell of an experience he had while a student of Dr. Graham Scroggie. The topic for discussion was prayer, and Dr. Scroggie was emphasizing how prayer was not an option in the life of the believer. Stephen asked him what you should do when you didn't feel like praying, to which Dr. Scroggie replied, "Stephen, pray when you feel like it; pray when you don't feel like it; pray until you do feel like it!"

Worship is not an option for the believer. It may or may not be accompanied by any great emotion, but it must be offered, because not to worship the God "who so loved" is not just an omission on the part of a child of God; it is an act of disobedience and is the epitome of arrogance and pride. *Worship is the natural, normal response to God the Creator from the heart of a grateful creature.*

Pastor and Director of Music, I am not saying that time needs to be given for corporate response to everything in a service, but I am saying that there are those moments when it is most appropriate. I will go so far as to say that some segments of a service may be left incomplete when they are just dropped, and no opportunity for reflection or response is given. Let me give you a few examples.

Paula has just finished singing the solo "Broken and Spilled Out," which expresses a profound message of death to her own will and absolute surrender of her life to God. This has been more than just the singing of a solo; it has been the prayer of one of God's children. What happens now? Tragically, in many churches today the congregation will applaud. Paula will go back to her seat in the choir, and the soprano sitting next to her will pat her on the leg and say, "That was beautiful, Paula." Paula will say, "Thank you." The minister of music will give her an affirming nod, and the pastor will say, "I always love to hear that song. Thank you, Paula." Or the pastor may not say anything but just go on to the next thing on the program agenda, and another opportunity for the worshipers to "do business" with God will have gone by the wayside in the name of expediency. A message in song will have become simply the performance of a song, and the impact that moment could have had in the lives of those listening, as Paula poured out her heart to the Lord, is lost.

On the other hand, the pastor might realize that God is speaking as Paula is singing. What can he do to help this be all God wants it to be? If Paula really means what she is singing, this is a profound moment in her life. But it might also be for the whole church. The impact this moment could have must not be emptied by applause, which the people, wanting to respond in some way, will probably do. The pastor prays silently, "Lord, this was not on our worship schedule, but it was on Yours. So I trust You to help me lead these— your people—in an appropriate response." As Paula concludes her solo, the pastor walks to the pulpit. Before the people can clap, he says: "We have just heard a message from the Lord. If we were really to take these words to heart, I believe this church, in all probability, would begin to experience the revival we have been praying for. I want to ask any of you who feel that you would like to turn this moment into a time of fresh surrender to the Lord, a time of asking Him to make you a vessel through whom the fragrance of His life can flow, to come and join me at the altar. If you wish, of course, you may stay right where you are to pray. And Paula, as we begin to pray, would you sing "Broken and Spilled Out" again, as each of us makes it our own personal prayer?" Though the pastor has a message to preach, he is sensitive to the fact that God was also speaking through another one of His children that morning, and he didn't want to miss what God was saying through Paula.

Times like this will not happen in every service, but opportunities like this are missed more often than we realize. It is not always necessary to make as big an adjustment as was made in the case of Paula's solo. Sometimes just a moment of Spirit-led response is sufficient to bring to completion what God is doing.

Here is another example. It is the "special" before the sermon. The choir is singing a medley of songs on the greatness of God that climaxes with "How Great Thou Art." The pastor knows that the congregation may applaud. If they do, the impact that this message in music could have will be dissipated. What should he do? He turns to Psalm 19; and as the music climaxes with the glorious declaration, "How Great Thou Art," he is at the pulpit. In the spirit of what has just happened, he says, "Please repeat after me: 'The heavens declare the glory of God;' (the congregation responds) 'And the firmament shows His handiwork.'" He goes through the entire fourteen verses of the psalm with the people repeating after him. As they repeat the last verse, "Let the words of my mouth and the meditation of my heart be acceptable in Your sight, O LORD, my strength and my Redeemer," he uses it as a prayer to lead into the message.

What would have been just another exciting anthem sung by the choir and appreciated by the congregation has now become more than special music, for the people have been led in response to their great God. That moment of worship through music was brought to completion by an appropriate response.

Let me give you another illustration. This has to do with our modeling appropriate responses for our children. When children minister through music, it often becomes a photo-shoot time for parents and grandparents and an aren't-they-cute moment in the service. Wanting to let the children know they are appreciated, nine times out of ten everybody applauds when they are through, without regard to what they actually were singing. The children feel good. The people liked what they did. They "performed" well, but is that all the children can learn from their experience? Would it not be more fitting for the pastor, rather than leading the congregation in applause, to take a moment to pray and thank God for the children, for those who work with them, for the message they brought to the church, and so on. Then, as they are going back to their seats, he could thank them for having served the Lord the way they did and for being a blessing to the church. By responding in this way, the focus remains on God and His work. The children know that what they have done is honoring to Him and appreciated by the people, and the children have been instructed in the ways of the Lord and worship.

Response is right. For a congregation to make the right response, however, will sometimes require help from the worship leaders. And just as worship is both private and public, the way we respond to God in private may not always be appropriate in a public worship setting. I may choose to do something when I am alone with God that would be a stumbling block to someone if I were to do it in public. There have been times that I have lain on my face before the Lord on the floor of my attic study, but if I were to do that in a Sunday morning worship service it would more often than not be a distraction. I do a lot of pacing in my private worship. There have been times that I have shouted at the top of my lungs when I have been on an early-morning run in the countryside. I would not do these things in church. To say that because David danced before the Lord in public means that in church we can do whatever we want, whenever we feel like it, is more likely a sign of spiritual *immaturity* than of spiritual *maturity*.

As leaders we need to be sensitive to the dynamics of corporate worship and not allow a well-meaning, zealous believer to disrupt the worship of the body. Remember that a word of correction or counsel will always be graciously received by a Spirit-filled Christian. Today, when much so-called worship is driven by adrenaline rather than by the Spirit, worship leaders need to continuously and carefully watch, pray, direct, and instruct in the wisdom and power of our Lord.

Remember that the "applause syndrome" of today is largely due to the "electronic church," which has introduced and perpetuated it in an atmosphere that is often more like "show biz" than like worship. Though there may be times when applause would be fitting, the fundamental question we need to be asking ourselves is not whether we should applaud in church but *how best to respond to God.*

Remember that there is a significant difference between responding to an individual in appreciation for what he has done and responding to the Lord for what He has done through them. Singer-musicians need to understand that they are not performing but are ministering truth and life to the people.

When week after week, month after month, year after year, the only response they get is a hand clap from the pastor, music director, and congregation, it is no wonder we have more performing today than ministering. No wonder we have all the gyrations occurring onstage that appeal more to the flesh and soul than to the spirit. When soloists are applauded for singing a prayer, no wonder they see it as performing a song rather than praying. When choirs and ensembles pour out their hearts to the Lord and the pastor says, "Wasn't that pretty," or, "Let's give them a hand," no wonder there is more glorifying of man's talent today than the glorifying of God!

Oh, Pastor, Director of Music, teach your people to discern what is right. Lead them, admonish them, model it for them. I recall a moment in a service at the European Baptist Convention's Summer Conference in Interlaken, Switzerland, in the summer of 1997 when a soloist sang. She sang so beautifully to the Lord. It was a prayer offered to Him from her heart. The moment she finished, however, and before I could get to the podium, the people broke into applause. I know they were expressing appreciation for her beautiful voice and the way she had sung, but this was not the time for applause. I remember so clearly debating in my mind whether just to go on or to offer a bit of counsel. I did the latter. I can't repeat verbatim what I said, but I do recall pointing out to them what Cecelia had just been doing. "She has just led us in prayer," I said. "She has been talking to God, but we were listening to it as the performance of a song. Do you applaud your pastor when he prays?" I asked. "Why is it that when a prayer is sung, we don't respond to it as a prayer? Because we see it as music," I continued, "and music is an art form. Therefore, we applaud." I prayed as I continued to speak that the people would not take offense at what I was saying but would hear my heart.

After the service I was overwhelmed at the response, as one after another came either to say that this affirmed their own convictions or that this was the first time anyone had led them to think of what they were doing. They had just applauded because everyone else did.

To applaud in worship? Perhaps, sometimes. To respond in worship? Yes! Always!

Preparing to
Worship

---

*When Jesus taught one of His most profound lessons, He was not in the synagogue,
nor was He addressing the religious leaders of that day. He was sitting on the side of
a well, talking to a Samaritan woman. "True worshipers will worship the Father in
spirit and truth; for the Father is seeking such to worship Him. God is Spirit, and
those who worship Him must worship in spirit and truth."*
—John 4:23b–24.

DEAR CHURCH STAFF,

Have you ever thought about what happens, or should I say, does not
happen in those moments just prior to the worship service in your church?
This has long been a concern of mine, for I believe the pre-service time should
be spent preparing ourselves to worship. It should be a time to pray, to read
Scripture, to get ready for what we are about to do.

We take time to prepare in other areas of our lives. We warm up before
participating in sporting events; we prepare for exams. Many do physical exercise before beginning their daily activities. But when it comes to worshiping
God, usually little thought is given to preparation.

This was originally the purpose for the instrumental prelude. The music
was intended to help the waiting worshipers collect their thoughts, focus on
God, and prepare their hearts to join together in offering their adoration,
thanksgiving, and praise to Him. It was never meant to be a background for
conversation. Yet that is exactly what happens in many of our evangelical
churches today.

As the people wait for the service to begin, they talk. And the talk is usually about everything except the things of God. We talk about our children, we

talk about sports, we talk about the weather, we talk about this and that. But seldom if ever do we talk about what we are about to do. Meanwhile the instrumentalist, who may have spent a good bit of time praying and preparing for the prelude, gets little if any attention. Those who might wish to listen have to do so over the din of a talking congregation.

Then, when it is time to begin, a worship leader calls the meeting to order, a "call to worship" may be sung or read, a hymn is announced, and everyone dutifully stands and goes through a perfunctory performance of something like "Holy, Holy, Holy," without having taken a moment to even think on the holiness of God. The hymn has little or no impact on those singing because the mind has not yet been engaged, let alone the heart. And so the words quickly fall from the lips—words so profound that, if the worshipers were prepared for them, they would be led not only to see God but also to see themselves in light of who He is.

In other churches, services may begin with some "wake-up" music— something rhythmic and upbeat to get the so-called worshipers' attention. Music becomes a tool to get people "in the mood to worship." The inherent danger in this is that people can easily become emotionally roused but not spiritually awakened. They sing without thinking. The body and emotions respond to the "feel" of the music, but the mind and will have not been engaged. Most church members have never considered the need of getting their minds and hearts ready for what they are there to do—to worship God. As I have said in another letter, worship is a response to who God is. When no time is given to focusing on God, either through Scripture or prayer, to what are the people responding? To God or to music? It is for this reason that I write this letter to you.

I believe that the pre-service time can be one of the most effective tools to help your people begin understanding what worship really is. Without drawing this letter out or belaboring the point, I want to make a few suggestions. As you pray about this, the Lord will show you additional ways to help your people become *worshipers*.

Those of you who have PowerPoint™ equipment or some kind of video setup have a wonderful tool for worship preparation. Most often, however, the equipment is used primarily—if not exclusively—to make announcements and promote programs. This in itself may be indicative of what is most important in the eyes of the church leadership. We have been in church services where at least ten minutes of the pre-service time was given to promotion of church activities on a screen. These same announcements were also printed in the church bulletin, and in many cases time would be taken in the service to make the announcements *again!*

In light of why the people have assembled in the first place—to worship God—why not devote at least part of the pre-service time to spiritually warming the congregants' hearts, getting them ready to do what they are there for? Here are some things you might consider.

1. *Using Scripture.* The Scripture verses could be from any part of the Bible, but the psalms are particularly full of rich portions to help turn one's focus to God. In addition to these, you might have your people turn to the passage of Scripture from which the pastor will be speaking. This will help them prepare for what God is going to say through His Word. In a day when so little time is given to the public reading of Scripture in our services—a subject I address in another letter—this can be of great spiritual benefit to your people.

2. *The Sermon Outline.* Pastor, if you do not wish to put your entire outline on the screen, you might consider putting down some salient thoughts for your people to be contemplating. This helps get your people thinking in the direction you want to lead them.

3. *Words of Great Hymns or Choruses.* This can be a very effective tool of preparation. Sometimes you could include the story behind the writing of one of our great hymns. What an inspiration this would be, especially if you are going to sing that hymn in the service.

4. *Prayers.* This part of the worship preparation might be preceded by an invitation to the congregation to pray silently. It could be a prayer for the pastor, for God's anointing and enabling as he leads in worship. It could include the other worship facilitators: music director, soloists, choir, instrumentalists, and so on. The prayer might also be for the congregation, that God would give them listening ears and an open heart. The prayer should include Scripture. This will take time in prayerful preparation but will surely reap great rewards.

Should it be necessary to also do some promotion, you might consider doing that first, then switching from announcements to worship preparation five minutes or so before the service begins. For a while you will need to have someone "coach" your people, someone to lead them to do what you want them to do. Otherwise, you will have half of the people talking while the other half is trying to prepare themselves to worship. It will take time for your people to change their habits. Another aid is to put the words of the prelude on the screen if it is an arrangement of a familiar hymn or chorus(es). This will help in engaging the mind.

For those churches that do not use multimedia during the pre-service time, I would like to make a few suggestions. These may be of use to you, or there may be other things that you feel would work better in your situation. Whatever it is, your goal is to help your people prepare to worship God.

1. *Print worship preparation helps in your bulletin.* This could be Scriptures for the people to read or a prayer that you ask them to pray for the pastor and other worship facilitators, as well as for themselves. It could be several soul-searching questions that you ask them to ask themselves before engaging in the act of worshiping God.

2. *Reading of Scripture.* Prior to the prelude, have someone lead the congregation in a reading of Scripture. This is a good time to read the full passage from which the sermon text will be taken. I like very much what the Hook Evangelical Church in the London, England, area does. This is the church where Brian Edwards, author of *Revival: A People Saturated with God,* served as pastor for many years. Five to ten minutes prior to the scheduled time for the service, one of the staff or a deacon stands at the pulpit, announces the topic of the morning's sermon, and asks those who are already seated to turn in their Bibles to the chapter pertaining to the message. At that point they will read the passage together out loud. They are led in prayer, then asked to meditate on the passage while the prelude is being played. When the people begin singing a few minutes later, they are ready to worship! This is a good time to involve some of your youth in Scripture reading. Insist that they practice the reading. Have them read it for you before time, pastor or other worship facilitator, to make sure that they can pronounce all the words correctly. Make this assignment an important one. This will establish the value you place on the public reading of God's Word.

Though I will address this in my letter to instrumentalists, I want to reiterate here that those who are responsible for the music prior to the service need to be very sensitive in choosing what they play. It is of utmost importance that the music be conducive to heart preparation and not sound either like the Academy Awards Ceremony, a baseball game, or a nightclub. *You are not playing to entertain; you are playing to help people prepare to worship.*

These are but a few suggestions, but I trust they will be helpful to you. The Lord may very well lead you to do some things that will be unique to your situation, which will lead your people to a deeper understanding of what worship is and the need to prepare themselves before participating in the highest calling and privilege we have as Christians—worshiping our God.

Building Continuity into a Service

Cutting the Trough So the Water Can Flow

The role of worship leaders is not to make the worshipers happy or to impress them with their abilities, but to help them encounter God. This involves helping them understand where they have been and where they are going.

DEAR PASTOR AND DIRECTOR OF MUSIC,

It may seem strange that I'm writing to you about "cutting a trough so the water can flow" in the context of worship. This phrase, however, is one which has been attributed to C. S. Lewis, and it depicts an often overlooked part of the assignment of the worship leader—the building of continuity into the service.

Over the years I've observed many services that seem to have been put together with little, if any, consideration of "flow," or connection. The choir special leads the thoughts of the people in one direction and the solo in another. Often the combination of hymns and choruses used follow no particular theme. They are simply a disjointed grouping of songs, and none of them may have anything to do with the message. The service is made up of an assortment of "minibites."

As a result, if you were to ask people after the service what it was about, they would be hard pressed to come up with a theme. They were never really led in any particular direction because no direction had been planned. Each worship leader prepared for his own area, with no knowledge of the direction the other would be going. Congregational songs were selected and sung, specials were performed, and the sermon was preached with no attempt to relate one to the other.

Can you imagine the outcome if two writers, collaborating on the creating of a play or musical, never communicated with one another? This, in fact, is what is happening in many of our churches when worship leaders are not working together in the building of the worship service. When the trough is not properly cut, the result is a service with no "flow."

"But I've always done it this way," one director of music said to me. "I pick songs the people like to sing, although I do try to teach them something new from time to time. The congregation always seems to enjoy the 'song service,' but I seldom think of what I do in music as needing to fit with anything else. I'm responsible for my part of the service, and the pastor for his."

When this is the scenario, the people will certainly have no sense of where they began or where they may be going. It requires little effort simply to select songs to sing, but *it takes time and prayer* to prepare a service that has continuity or "sequential thrust." Unless the pastor leads the music himself, he will have to spend time with the music director. Together they will need to discuss the general theme, their beginning point, what specials will be sung, which Scriptures will be used, and the topics for public prayer. They will choose the most appropriate "commitment" hymn or closing song that will best express a response to the content of the message. Finally, they will decide how everything will be tied together in order to facilitate the congregants in their worship of God and to prepare their hearts for the receiving of God's Word.

We should never be satisfied with hodgepodge. We should do everything we can to help our people really worship and not just sing songs, listen to prayers being prayed, and hear a sermon preached.

Many times over the years we've had people come up to us following a service that we have been privileged to lead and say: "That made sense. I've never seen it done that way before." In further discussion they would share how it had helped them to worship. For some, it was the first time they were able to see the purpose for what had been done and to understand what was happening. One part of the service led directly to the next, as Scriptures, prayers, comments, message, and music were tied together. With planning and prayer you can make it much easier for your people to "draw near to God" in worship. (See the "Checklist for Worship Leaders" in the Appendix.)

Now for one final thought. It is sometimes necessary to help your people transition from one part of the service to another. There are times when the flow of a service is going quite naturally and no transition is necessary. There are other occasions, however, when a few words of bridging from what has taken place to what is going to happen can make a great deal of difference to your people's understanding of what is going on.

I've often observed worship leaders plunge into "their part" of the service as though nothing of significance had occurred up to that point. This seems to happen most often with pastors or other speakers who, though not saying it or necessarily meaning it, act as though what has gone on before their message is irrelevant. This is never more apparent than when the pastor or guest speaker gets up following music that has really spoken to people's hearts and immediately undoes all that has been done by telling a joke. The people immediately "forget" what just took place, as their focus shifts from worship to the speaker. What this communicates is that what has already taken place really has not been important.

I am writing to admonish you not to let something fall by the wayside by acting as though it had not even taken place. I believe that such insensitivity, even when it is unintentional, grieves the Holy Spirit. The role of worship leaders is not just one of announcing page numbers or waving arms; it is a spiritual one. It is the assignment of the worship leadership to help the worshipers along, to guide them, to help them assimilate and participate with understanding. It is our assignment to assist them to respond in their hearts, sometimes even physically and audibly, when a response is appropriate.

The role of worship leaders is not to make the worshipers happy or impress them with their ability but to help the people encounter God. This involves helping them understand where they have been and where they are going. It is not difficult, but it takes mental alertness and spiritual sensitivity. Picking up a phrase of a song that has just been sung and using it to bridge into what comes next does not sound like anything out of the ordinary, but in doing so, you are showing the people that what has just taken place had a purpose and that what is going to follow will lead them on from that point. An unscheduled, impromptu prayer or a verse of Scripture may be the appropriate thing to do at times. The inserting of a chorus or hymn that may not have been planned can do much toward making a moment in the service "extra" ordinary.

In the final analysis, your role as worship leader is simply doing everything you can to help, and not hinder, your people in meeting God. It requires sensitivity to what the Spirit of God may be doing each time the people meet together to worship.

To the Choir

---

*A choir member is both a worshiper and a worship facilitator.
As with all worship leaders, the choir's role is to glorify God
and to help the congregation encounter Him in worship.*

Dear Choir,

What a heritage you have! In addition to the hundreds of references to music and song, direct references to "singers" abound throughout Scripture. In 1 Chronicles 15 we read of the formal organizing of a choir by order of David, "to sing joyful songs. . . ." (v. 16 NIV). Chenaniah, the head Levite who "was skillful," was assigned to be "in charge of the singing" (v. 22 NIV). Nehemiah had a specific function, relating to the building of the wall, for the choirs he had organized. The pronouncement of our Lord's birth to the shepherds was accompanied by a great heavenly host glorifying God. We know this great heavenly host continues to worship and glorify God in heaven as we read in the Revelation of "ten thousand times ten thousand, and thousands of thousands, saying . . . 'Worthy is the Lamb'" (Rev. 5:11–12). And one day, *all* of God's redeemed will be singing that anthem, when singers and those who thought they would never be able to carry a tune will join the hosts of heaven to sing in perfect tone and harmony. What a choir that will be!

Until that time comes, the assignment of the church choir remains essentially as it has been throughout Scripture and as we know it will be in eternity future—to declare the marvelous works of God and to magnify Him. This is it! This was why those skilled with singing ability in Scripture were set apart.

There was no other reason. The singers of the nations around Israel would sing "their" songs, but the choirs of God's people would sing only of their God.

Since biblical days, some of the most glorious music written has been written "out of Scripture" for choir, by both church and secular composers. The Bach cantatas and oratorios, Handel's *Messiah*, plus thousands of other examples show people attempting to interpret through music, especially for choir, the message of the Bible. Beethoven's Ninth and final symphony climaxes with the glorious "Ode to Joy" for choir, soloists, and orchestra. We know it in our hymnals as "Joyful, Joyful, We Adore Thee."

The church choir set the pace and standard for the other types of choirs that would follow. Though these other choirs sang all kinds of music, the church choirs always sang the message of Scripture. It was for this reason and this reason alone that it has existed over the centuries—to sing "of Him, through Him, and to Him." That is, until recent years when the church began to leave its first love. Its leaving began to be reflected in the singing of "other" songs by the choir.

It is interesting to note, in looking back across the history of the church, how often the music pictured the spiritual state of the church. When the church was in a period of apostasy, it turned more and more to drama and entertainment. (I speak of this more fully in *When Church Was Just Church* in the Appendix.) But when the church turned back to God, preaching was restored to its rightful place, and the return was reflected in its music. The church choirs no longer had to entertain to keep the people interested. A revived people did not want to be entertained when they came to church.

What does this say about us today? Entertainment is on the ascendancy in the American church. It has, in fact, just about taken over some of our churches. Millions of dollars are spent annually on pageants that reap little spiritual fruit. The week-to-week productions performed in our buildings built as theaters have turned many church choirs into entertainment organizations. Could this be a sign that we have left our first love?

Choir, you do not exist to entertain. You exist to sing to the glory of God alone. You exist to assist the church in its worship of Him. It is no light matter to have the assignment you have. It is no light matter to be worship facilitators. Choir Member, you are not in the choir for music's sake. God's purpose for you and the choir is a much higher one than that. You are not there to please yourself or the people—you are there to please God. This should affect your commitment to take the time to rehearse. It should affect how you live, for you are representing God in the role He has given you. This will affect your relationships with others in the choir, because broken relationships create disharmony.

A correct understanding of your responsibility will cause you to do everything you can to keep unity because you want God to be able to bless. You will not allow jealousy or bitterness to get a hold on you, because these will eventually destroy your usefulness and will work like leaven to ruin any spiritual impact the choir could make. As I've said in several of my letters to others on the worship team, we are all members of a body, and it is God's will and purpose that we function as a healthy body for His glory.

There are many other things that I would like to say, but I will keep them for another letter. I want to say a word, however, to the small church choir, the choir that may think it is somewhat "less" than the choir in the larger church across town. You cannot do the music they do. You do not have the trained singers they do. You are not on television. Your accompanist is limited in the pieces she can play. You could go on and on listing reasons you are not as good as some other choirs. Well, this may all be true, but let me give you this word of encouragement.

You have all the ingredients needed to offer God acceptable worship and to please Him. To people's ears you may not sound as good as the other choir, but what is really important is not how the choir sounds to people; it is how it sounds to God. As I have said in other letters, with God, it is fundamentally a matter of the heart. If the offering you make in song to God on a Sunday morning is offered from hearts that love Him supremely, the sound to God's ears is more excellent than the sound of the greatest choir in the land whose offering may be rejected because they are doing it for themselves, for the pleasure it gives them, rather than doing it for God.

I sometimes imagine God as having a huge celestial sound conversion system that receives all that is offered in Spirit and in truth on earth. No matter how it may sound down here, when it reaches His ears it has been transformed into the sound that only the choir of His redeemed can make. And it is true music to His ears.

I want to leave you with this "paraphrase for choir," taken from several psalms. I pray that you will keep this before you as a description of your ministry assignment.

Sing to the Lord, choir; sing to the Lord and praise His name.
Proclaim His salvation and declare His glory every time you sing.
Sing of the Lord's marvelous deeds, for He is great and worthy of praise.
When you sing, choir, remember that splendor and majesty are before Him,
and strength and glory fill His sanctuary.

When you sing, choir, never fail to ascribe to Him the glory that is due His name.
Worship the Lord, choir, in the beauty of His holiness, and help the people
understand that He is a great God, that they are the sheep of His pasture.

Lead God's people, choir, to kneel before the Lord their Maker,
the One who is robed
in holiness, whose throne has been established for all eternity.
When you sing, choir, sing to the Lord; sing to the Lord;
sing always and only to the Lord!

To the Soloist

A prayer of David, a servant-soloist:
O God, You are my God;
Early will I seek You;
My soul thirsts for You;
My flesh longs for You
In a dry and thirsty land
Where there is no water.
So I have looked for You in the sanctuary,
To see Your power and Your glory.
Because Your lovingkindness is better than life,
My lips shall praise You.
Thus I will bless You while I live;
I will lift up my hands in Your name.
My soul shall be satisfied as with marrow and fatness,
And my mouth shall praise You with joyful lips.
—Psalm 63:1–5

DEAR SOLOIST,

As I write this letter, I am thinking of all singers and musicians who, either individually or in an ensemble, use the vehicle of music to convey a message from the Lord to a congregation or lead the listeners to focus their minds and hearts on the Lord.

Soloists, we are first of all ministers, and our ministry is first of all *to God*, then to the people. We are not there to entertain or even to perform a musical number. When we stand before the people, we represent the One who has chosen us to be part of "a royal priesthood, a holy nation, His own special people, that [we] may proclaim the praises of Him who called [us] out of darkness into His marvelous light" (1 Pet. 2:9). It is for Him and about Him that we are playing or singing. We are not there to represent or promote ourselves; we are there to represent and promote God. We are not there to impress the people with how wonderful our talent is but to impress the people with how wonderful our God is.

In light of this, we must be ever so careful that we don't do anything to detract from our calling and mission. First of all, we must be careful how we look. That means, *be careful how you dress.* Some singers, by just the way they appear, are saying, "Look at me!" Any distractingly loud or sensual attire has no place in the context of worship. (Actually, it should not have any place in the life of a child of God at any time.) There have been times that I have been embarrassed at what some singer/musician was wearing as she stood before the people. In my letter in this book on the third commandment, I pointed out that anything done "in the name of Jesus" must be in the character of that name. When we dress in any way that is out of character with who Jesus is, we are misusing the name of our Lord. Though we live in the world, we are not to be shaped by it. Dear fellow soloist, the first impression people get of you is how you look. The way you dress can cancel out what you sing or play. Be careful how you dress!

Secondly, *be careful how you move!* What is done with body movements can speak as loudly as the music. The rule of thumb is, don't do anything that distracts from your purpose in standing before the people. You are a representative of God. What you do with your body will either support the message or detract from it. Unnecessary use of your hands can be a distraction. Putting on a show with the rest of your body, which is not unusual these days, does nothing to glorify the Lord. Caressing the microphone as though you were doing a nightclub act is not in the character of our Lord. You are not there to show yourself off; you are there to show the people something about God. You, in essence, are the face of God to the people before whom you are standing. So be careful how you move. How spiritually satisfying it is to watch singers who are visually supportive of the message they are declaring in song. Your body and your eyes are as much a part of the harmony of the song as are the words and music.

This brings me to something that has been a major concern of mine for years. It is a phenomenon that is found primarily, if not almost exclusively, in the Western church, by which I mean Western Europe, the United States, and Canada. This phenomenon is evidence of how much the entertainment spirit of the world has pressed the church into its mold. In the world, words set to music become an "art form." This art form, called "song," takes on all kinds of shapes and sounds. No matter how it sounds, however, its purpose is to entertain. The singer sings to and for an audience. What concerns me is how much Christian singers and musicians of our day think the same way. A song is seen as an art form, albeit Christian, that is to be performed for an audience. This often leads to a disregard of what the words are saying, since the words have become subservient to the art form. No longer is the music primarily a vehicle to carry the message of the words, but the two have now become a song to sing. And often the song does not portray the true meaning of the words.

Let me illustrate what I mean by using an example from a Christian television special I watched some time ago. The program was an hour of "golden oldies" sung by a number of "oldies." (I do not say this with any disrespect because I could have easily blended in with the rest!) All of these singers were well-known and have been a blessing to thousands of people over the years. But as I watched, this phenomenon surfaced a number of times during that hour. It happened when they were singing "How Great Thou Art." You recall that the first stanza and refrain are a prayer, words addressed to God. As I listened and watched the singers singing the prayer, however, I saw them treating the prayer as an art form and not as a prayer. Yes, they were singing the words. But as they were mouthing the words of a prayer to God, they were smiling, looking at each other, and several times patted each other on the back. They were having what the British would call "a jolly good time." When they finished, they congratulated each other, while the rest of the group who had been listening applauded the performance of a song. "How Great Thou Art" had been reduced to an art form. They had been singing the words of a prayer, yet its message seemed to be far from their minds.

Sadly, this happens all too frequently in our churches. Soloists stand to sing the words of a prayer but treat the prayer as an art form. As they sing some prayer, they look at the "audience" and smile. Their eyes and body are saying to the people, "I am singing a song for you," while with their lips they are talking to God. The congregation has become the focus of their singing. The people have become the audience of their prayer rather than God. So why should we be surprised when the people applaud our prayer?

Why does this concern me? It concerns me because I believe that in doing this we are breaking the third commandment. We are misusing the name of God. We have reduced to an art form the awesome right and privilege we have as His children to pray to Him. This may come close to what happened over and over again in the life of the children of Israel, when they were going through the form of worship yet their hearts were far from Him. On one of these occasions, God told them that, even though they were lifting their hands to Him in prayer, He would not hear them. God's name is no less sacred to Him today than it was in that day; our praying to Him is no less holy than it was back then. How quickly we can make common that which God has declared to be holy!

What can we do about it? Let's wake up and return to the reality of what we are really doing when we sing. If you are singing a prayer, ask the congregation to bow their heads as you pray. Or, if it is your custom to close your eyes when you pray, close your eyes. Don't let a voice teacher tell you that you should never do that when you sing. That may be true if you are performing; but, fellow singer, we are not performers. If you choose not to close your eyes or have the people bow their heads, your eyes should be turned upward. In this way your eyes will communicate what you are saying in your words. You are there to minister to God and to the people. Don't let anyone persuade you that you always have to make eye contact with your "audience." *If you are talking to God with your lips, don't talk to the people with your eyes.* If you are addressing the people, then look at them.

Over the years we have found this to be a strong teaching tool for the congregations we've been privileged to minister to. It underlines what you are really doing and helps them participate in their own spirits.

Finally, *be careful how you sing, Singers!* I am not speaking primarily now of voice training because we live in a day when singing technically well is not always a requirement. This is not to say that as Christians we should ever be content to offer God anything less than the best we have. I believe this includes taking the talent God has invested in us and developing it to its maximum potential for Him. The parable of the "talents" is as applicable to musicianship as it is to anything else. However, with the advent of sophisticated sound systems with all their enhancement possibilities, we now can actually sound *better* than we are! Yet as helpful as this may be, it opens up the possibility of overdoing it. I've listened to singers who have left me more impressed with their sound effects than with God. When this happens, we have failed in our assignment as ambassadors of Christ.

It is so easy to do something that is more of a distraction from God than an attraction to Him. This can happen when you use an accompaniment track that distracts from the message rather than enhances it, either because of its being played too loudly or its being overarranged. Your track should not distract! It is entirely possible to have such a bad "marriage" between the music and the words that the message is canceled out by the music.

Representing God to the people is an awesome responsibility. To use our talents in a way that honors Him takes much prayer, time in His Word, and a daily humbling of ourselves before Him. At times it will require refraining from doing something musically that may be "lawful" but not "expedient," as the apostle Paul put it. Just because you can hit a high note does not mean that you should sing one at the end of every song. There will be times when that is exactly what should be done to enhance the message. There will be times, however, when the high note will be more of an exhibition of your vocal prowess than an exhibition of God's glory. I heard a music evangelist say one day, "If you've got it, flaunt it." I hope he was saying that in jest.

I have been present when singers or instrumentalists have beautifully led the listeners to the feet of the Master, right up to the last phrase or two of the song, when suddenly they did something that immediately drew our attention to them and their abilities and away from thinking about God. How quickly ministry can be turned into performance. How quickly we can move from being a highway to God to being an obstacle in the way. *How quickly we can turn from using our talent to display God to using God to display our talent.*

How quickly we can become proud of what we can do or of how we sound. That is why we singers and musicians must be extrasensitive to apply the cross daily to our lives. In Galatians 6:14, the apostle Paul said that if you want to boast in something don't boast or take pride in what you have achieved but boast in the cross of Jesus and what it has done for you. The implications of this are enormous, for the cross always symbolized death. Anyone who "took up his cross" was headed down a road from which there was no return. The line was drawn. There was no room for negotiation. The cross would not accept any truce or compromise. Any urge to bask in the sunlight of man's acclamation was dissolved by the shadow of the cross.

The world will tempt you to think that the cross is meant to be applied only to certain areas of your life and certainly not to your music career. But the Bible says that we are to always have the attitude of Christ, who "humbled Himself and became obedient to the point of death, even the death of the cross" (Phil. 2:8).

If the cross has really touched your life, it has put you out of joint with this world, out of joint with any desire to seek the applause and acclamation of men. It has, as someone put it, "wounded your thigh, and you ought to be praising God every time you limp." If you want to boast, don't boast in what you have done or in what you can do. If you want to boast, don't boast in what people may say about you. If you want to boast, don't boast in how much you think God is using you and blessing your ministry. *Be thankful, but boast in the cross!*

Isaac Watts summed it up in these profound words: "Forbid it, Lord, that I should boast, Save in the death of Christ, my God. All the vain things that charm me most, I sacrifice them to His blood."[1]

Dear Fellow Singer/Musician, let us boast, let us glory, but let it be only "in the cross of our Lord Jesus Christ, by whom the world has been crucified to [us], and [we] to the world" (Gal. 6:14).

To the Accompanists

Then David spoke to the leaders of the Levites
to appoint their brethren to be the singers
accompanied by instruments of music.
—1 Chronicles 15:16

DEAR ACCOMPANISTS,

I am writing this letter primarily to keyboard musicians who, in most of our churches, still carry the main responsibility for accompanying congregational singing and specials, playing preludes, offertories, and postludes, as well as a variety of other spur-of-the-moment assignments. I am writing to those in whose hands has been placed the musical responsibility to provide the kind of atmosphere that will help people worship. For you to understand this letter, however, you will need to keep in mind the "worship context" I have been writing about in previous letters—worship as we find it modeled and defined in Scripture.

First of all, you are part of a "worship team." The team may consist of only a few, or it may number in the hundreds. No matter what the size may be, you are the underpinning for much that will take place in the service, from the prelude to the postlude. And no matter how little training you may have had or how proficient you may feel yourself to be, your assignment is most significant.

As has every other member of the worship team, you have been called of God to minister first to Him, then to the people. As were the musicians of the Old Testament, you have been set apart and assigned to glorify God and to help the people encounter Him in worship. You are not there to display your talent; your assignment is to display God through the talent He has given you. There is, therefore, no place for ego and pride. And conversely, there is no place for feeling sorry for yourself because you may not have had the opportunity to study as much as others and may feel you are not as accomplished a musician as you wish you were. If you are offering God the best you have, that is all He asks of you. After all, *God's eyes are on your heart,* not on your fingers. Across town people may be "oohing" and "aahing" at the talent of their piano player. They may be lining up to congratulate him on the fantastic offertory he played, while God may not have been at all impressed. On the other hand, no one may have said anything about the offertory you played that morning. No one may have been impressed—except God. As you played, He knew how much you had practiced to do it as well as you did. And as you played, He knew how dependent you were on Him to get through it without making too many mistakes. As you played, He knew that you wanted first of all to please Him. And you did!

In addition to your assignment at the keyboard, there is the added dimension, as is true with the other members of the worship team, of working together in unity. It takes a lot of God's grace sometimes just to put up with what you have to. It doesn't take long to discover that Christians aren't perfect. It is, however, lamentable that the worst sometimes comes out in the context of the church, and often within the music ministry. Though we may be extremely creative in defending ourselves and coming up with all kinds of reasons for what we do and say, if it contributes to "dissonance" rather than "harmony," we are "playing" into the hand of the enemy. Within the ministry of church music there is the need to die daily to ourselves. And God seems to give us many opportunities to choose whether to do that.

One of these areas that is exceedingly sensitive, yet needs to be faced, is knowing when to "step down" or "move over." I have encountered this over the years on numerous occasions, when the time has really come for the piano or organ player to step back and allow someone else to pick up that assignment. But because there has developed such an identification with that position over the years, she is unwilling to let go, and it becomes a point of tension within the ministry. It takes the grace and wisdom of God to recognize when to step aside. What we must keep ever before us, however, is that we are not stepping out of usefulness to God, because He will always have another assignment for us within the body. This servant attitude of heart and mind that we are to exhibit is spelled out for us in the description of our Lord, who "made Himself of no reputation, taking the form of a bondservant" (Phil. 2:7).

I want to share a few observations and suggestions with you that I hope will stimulate your thinking as they relate to the many areas of your assignment. First of all comes the prelude. Traditionally, this has been a time for heart preparation, a time for "tuning," as it were. Over the years, however, in many churches it has become a time for the instrumentalists to play an accompaniment for talkers. It might be better named a "Prelude for Conversation" rather than a "Prelude for Meditation." I have addressed this more fully in another letter, but I thought I would include it also in this letter to you, because you are at the very heart of it. In addition to your prayerfully choosing something that will help the people begin focusing on the One they have come to worship, you might consider, at least from time to time, introducing what you will be playing with a word about the piece itself. If it is an arrangement of a hymn or hymns, you could share some of the words with them. Or if the church uses overhead projection, have the words put on the screen. For a change, you could simply project a Scripture that relates to what you will be playing. This is much better than just telling them not to talk. Sheep are led, not driven. One more thing about the prelude—it should always set a tone of worship and not make the congregation feel as though they were at a sports event.

Another area I want to say a word about has to do with your hymn accompaniments. The emphasis should always be on *accompaniment*. The instruments are to be both a guide for and an encouragement to the singing. Accompaniments, by their very nature, are a support for the main thing, and the main thing in this case is the singing of the congregation. The accompaniment should never drown out the singing, yet I have seen this happen many times, especially by an organ or orchestra. I've been in services where the more accurate description for what was happening would have been "Instruments with Congregational Accompaniment." When this happens, the singers can barely hear themselves singing, and they tend to pull back rather than sing louder. Many just stop singing to listen. I am not saying that there are never occasions for the organ to pull out all the stops. I recall those times when, after having been accompanied by the instruments for several stanzas of hymns such as "A Mighty Fortress Is Our God" or "All Hail the Power of Jesus' Name," all the stops were pulled out on the last stanza, and the entire place was carried heavenward on the wings of music and message.

There is one final thing I want to say in relation to congregational accompaniments. This has to do with the harmonies you use. When the people are singing, the accompanying chords used should be those that lend themselves to natural harmonizing by the voices. How often I have joined other believers in song and wished to sing the tenor line written in the hymnal or recorded in my mind, but the instrumentalist(s) was playing some "creative" harmonization that made it impossible. This may very well have been suitable for a solo special but did not help the people sing anything other than the melody. I believe this, along with music illiteracy and unfamiliarity with the hymns of the church, is one of the reasons we hear so little harmony singing in the American church. What a contrast it is to worship with believers in other countries, where many of the men would "rather die" than be caught singing the melody line.

Throughout all we do as worship leaders, there must be a constant sensitivity to what is happening in the service. There may be times when what you had planned to play for an offertory or postlude will not fit what the Holy Spirit has been doing in a service. For example: If just prior to the offering something has happened that has brought a deep solemnity over the congregation, but you had planned to play some rhythmic, upbeat piece for the offertory, the spiritually sensitive thing for you to do might be to set that aside for another time and turn to a hymn or chorus that would support rather than interfere with what is happening. This goes as well for the postlude. On more than one occasion I have witnessed the "relieving of conviction" occur when an instrumentalist or choir has done some bombastic closing number before people at the altar were even back to their seats. Some of the most meaningful offertories and postludes are those which present a very simple setting of a chorus or hymn that "fits."

God does not want us to feel constricted in our service to Him, but He does call us to be sensitive and willing to make adjustments. Some cannot be as flexible as others. That's all right. God does not ask us to do what we cannot do. He may, however, surprise us, as we learn more and more to depend on Him, as we mature in our understanding of His ways. Serve Him with joy! Rejoice in His calling on your life! Play your instrument—not only with your fingers but also with your heart!

To Audiovisual Ministers

For as we have many members in one body, but all the
members do not have the same function, so we, being many, are one body in Christ,
and individually members of one another.
—Romans 12:4–5

DEAR AUDIOVISUAL MINISTERS,

Though some of you may not see yourselves as an integral part of the worship team, nothing could be further from the truth. Just as is true in so many areas of life, what goes on behind the scenes at church has as much to do with the ministry as what is happening out front. This is in fact exactly the way God has set up the church to work. Scripture compares the church to a body made up of many members, with each member functioning as part of the whole for the good of the whole.

There was a day in which the audiovisual world was basically limited to what you saw and heard. There were no sound systems and special lighting. Though this is still true in some parts of the world, it is no longer so where you live and minister. Your part of the "body" has been expanding very rapidly in recent years, and your assignment, in many churches, has become indispensable.

This letter is not primarily about the mechanics of your ministry, since I know very little about those, yet at the same time it is indirectly related. In my association with audiovisual ministers over the years, I have sensed from time to time that they saw their function as primarily being one of technologists. In my interactions with some in your field of expertise, I've been told that there is a proclivity for this among you. I have also observed that people often look at you in this light, as the ones who "run the sound" or "operate the lights and video," and nothing more. This concerns me, for you are much more than the ones who sit there with your fingers on a lever, your "phones" on your ears, and your eyes on a monitor. When I am speaking or singing, or when Patricia is at the keyboard playing and singing, you are there with us. Though we are first and foremost dependent on the Holy Spirit for His enabling and anointing, we are at the same time looking to you, as part of the team and part of the body, to work with us in doing everything we can to make a clear, undisturbed declaration of God's Word.

I've also observed that the audiovisual ministers are not often included in prayer times before the service. Not only are they not invited to participate in this time, but I've noticed that they are seldom even prayed for. I am thankful for exceptions to this, and I can assure you that Patricia and I have been faithful to pray for you because we've experienced the good and the bad! There have been times when an unalert sound person has caused me, I admit, great frustration when a microphone that was to have been left on for Patricia at the piano has been turned off and not noticed until halfway through a duet. Then suddenly it is turned on at such high volume that the sound distorts, and all is lost.

Audiovisual Ministers, how important it is that you "breathe" with us. How important it is that nothing is allowed to distract the people from the business at hand. The slightest "hiccup," such as something being turned on too late or a track being played too loudly, can become a distraction that turns the focus of people's hearts and minds away from what God is doing.

I remember once being near the end of a service in which there was a real sense of the Lord's presence when suddenly, all the lighting in the sanctuary was changed. The "houselights" were dimmed, a "spot" was turned on me, and I couldn't see a thing. Not only was I disoriented, but I had lost the congregation's attention. Although we had specifically asked that the lighting be set as it would be for a normal worship service, our request was not followed. Later I learned that one of the "technicians" decided that because I was singing at that point, it would be best to turn the situation into a "concert" atmosphere. They succeeded, and the moment of worship was lost.

Remember that your assignment is vital to us. We work together, the "seen" and the "unseen." Our mission is one—to glorify God. It will require prayer, preparation, awareness, and alertness to succeed in our mission and to arrive at our goal. It will also take a servant heart, for not only are we serving each other, but we are also serving the Lord. Thank you for serving with us.

Returning to Worship

---

*Worship is that which ascribes to God His worth and
surrenders to Him in light of Who He is,
in light of His self-revelation in Scripture.*

DEAR WORSHIP LEADERS,

What a tragedy it is when God's people go through the motions of worship, yet what they do is not acceptable to Him. In many ways, this describes a large portion of the church today. As I have pointed out to you in the letters I have written, we have departed from God in many ways.

It seems that, when considering worship today, we're often more prone to begin with man than with God. We ask, "What do the people want?" Someone suggests we do a survey to see what kind of music they like. If this is where we start with worship, we are sure to miss the mark. Worship begins with God, and our view of Him determines the kind of worship we offer. What we like may give us a good feeling, but in light of Scripture, is it what God requires?

Throughout the Old Testament we find that the heart of God's people was reflected in their worship. The more their hearts turned away from God and they incorporated the gods of the nations around them into their worship, the more they sounded and looked like the world. These people, who had been called by God to be a "kingdom of priests and a holy nation" (Exod. 19:6), eventually became so accustomed to their substitute gods that they didn't even miss God when He withdrew His presence. They simply went on with the mechanics of their worship services. They were still God's people, but He was not with them. In Jeremiah 2, we hear God saying, "Neither did [my people] say, 'Where is the LORD, Who brought us up out of the land of Egypt . . . ?' The [pastors] did not say, 'Where is the LORD?' And those who handle the law [teachers] did not know Me. . . . Has a nation changed its gods, Which are not gods? But My people have changed their Glory For what does not profit" (vv. 6, 8, 11).

This pattern of departing from God occurred repeatedly, and it always resulted in God's disciplining of His people. At one point He sent them into seventy years of captivity to the Babylonians. In another case, recorded in Isaiah 1, they again were suffering from spiritual drunkenness and Godless thinking, and God calls the leaders "rulers of Sodom" and the "people of Gomorrah" (v. 10). He went on to say, "Incense is an abomination to Me" (v. 13). He could not endure their "sacred meeting" (v. 13), and He said He would hide His eyes from them when they lifted their hands to Him in prayer. He said, "Even though you make many prayers, I will not hear" (v. 15).

In this my final letter to you, I want to draw your attention to two examples of corporate worship in the Old Testament. In each case Israel has turned away from God, and we find the king, the leader of God's people, leading them back. And it all takes place in the context of worship.

The first example is recorded in 2 Chronicles 15:1–19, where we find Asa leading Judah in specific steps in returning to God and to the kind of worship that He required. After listening to God speak and taking heart at the promise of God's blessing if they would return, King Asa began to remove things from the life of the nation that were not honoring to God. This is where we, too, must begin in our return to worship. We want God to bless us, but often we are reluctant to get rid of the things that get in the way of His blessing. There are idols of the world in our lives that are a constant reminder of our unwillingness really to listen to God and make changes. There are things in our worship that may not be honoring to Him. The changes may not be easy or popular, yet they must be made.

Not only did Asa remove those things that were dishonoring to God; he took the next step of restoring the altar of the Lord that had been neglected and was in desperate need of repair. I think you would agree that you don't have to look long at the North American church today to see what bad shape the prayer altar is in. The church today spends more time at the altars of buildings, pageants, and programs than at the altar of prayer.

In the process of Judah's returning to God, an interesting thing began to happen. Many began to leave the Northern Kingdom of Israel to join the Southern Kingdom of Judah when they saw that the glory of the Lord was returning to His people. You might say that they were tired of the substitute altars and the gimmickery of man and longed for genuine worship.

After the altar was rebuilt, King Asa then led the entire nation in a time of worship, during which thousands of sheep and oxen were offered to the Lord in gratitude to Him. He didn't stop there, however. We find him leading his people to enter into covenant with the Lord to seek Him from that point on with all their heart and soul. They then brought back into the house of the Lord the dedicated things such as the silver, gold, and utensils that should have remained there all along. They had now *returned to worship.*

The second example of worship being at the heart of a nation's turning away from God and their returning to Him begins with the downfall of King Uzziah, who "when he was strong his heart was lifted up, to his destruction, for he transgressed against the LORD his God by entering the temple of the LORD to burn incense on the altar of incense" (2 Chron. 26:16). After having reigned so magnificently for fifty years, he spent his latter days in suffering and disgrace as a leper. Pride had entered his heart, and he had decided he could worship God any way he wanted. He tried, and he paid for it. You remember, of course, it was out of what happened to Uzziah that Isaiah met God in his life-changing worship encounter.

Jotham, Uzziah's son, then became king. He reigned for sixteen years and did what was right in God's sight. He in turn was followed by King Ahaz, who for the next sixteen years led God's people away from Him. "King Ahaz became increasingly unfaithful to the LORD. . . . He sacrificed to the gods of Damascus. . . . Ahaz gathered the articles of the house of God, cut in pieces the articles of the house of God, shut up the doors of the house of the LORD, and made for himself altars in every corner of Jerusalem. And in every single city of Judah he made high places to burn incense to other gods, and provoked to anger the LORD God of his fathers" (2 Chron. 28:22–25).

This was the state of affairs that Ahaz's son, Hezekiah, inherited when he ascended to the throne. But unlike his father, for the next twenty-nine years he walked in the ways of God and led the people of God back to Him. (Again notice that this takes place in the context of worship.) Hezekiah began with the restoration of true worship to the nation. He knew that when true worship was restored, when a correct view of God was restored to the people, their worship would be reflected in the way they lived. Worship and life are inseparable. How often have you heard someone say that they keep their "religion" private? It is this kind of philosophy that is behind the extreme interpreting of "the separation of church and state" to mean that personal beliefs must not influence the way our president, cabinet, congress, supreme court, and other officials make decisions. This reveals a basic ignorance and disorientation to what being a Christian is. It is regrettable but true that this is how some of our leaders who profess to be Christians actually feel. How different things would be if those who name the name of Christ would judge and govern according to God's revelation, and not according to opinion polls. As I have said before, worship cannot be separated from life!

We find in chapter 29 of 2 Chronicles that change began with the leaders. Hezekiah first called on the worship leaders, the Levites, to sanctify "themselves." If we are going to see a return to true corporate worship, it must begin with the leaders. "Hear me, Levites! Now sanctify yourselves, sanctify the house of the LORD God of your fathers, and carry out the rubbish from the holy place" (2 Chron. 29:5).

Hezekiah then told the Levites to sanctify (cleanse) the house of the Lord. After removing all the debris, they cleansed "the altar of burnt offerings with all its articles, and the table of the showbread with all its articles" (v. 18).

Before true worship can be restored to our individual lives and the corporate worship of the church, anything that is not of God, which is *debris* in His sight, will have to be removed. Do you see why a "revived people" and a "return to true worship" are synonymous? People who are offering God acceptable worship are people who are spiritually in tune with God.

Now that the cleansing had been completed, they were ready to offer God worship that would be acceptable to Him. "Then King Hezekiah rose early, gathered the rulers of the city [Jerusalem], and went up to the house of the LORD. And they brought seven bulls, seven rams, seven lambs, and seven male goats for a sin offering for the kingdom, for the sanctuary, and for Judah. Then he commanded the priests, the sons of Aaron, to offer them on the altar to the LORD. . . . And the priests killed them; and they presented their blood on the altar as a sin offering to make an atonement for all Israel, for the king commanded that the burnt offering and the sin offering be made for all Israel" (vv. 20–21, 24).

Having cleansed the altar, made the sin offerings, and sprinkled the blood of the animals on the altar, the nation was corporately ready to worship God. King Hezekiah now stationed the Levites in the house of the Lord. The Levites and priests stood with the instruments of David. Then the king ordered them to offer the burnt offering, which had been described to earlier generations as "an offering made by fire, a sweet aroma to the Lord" (Lev. 1:9). Now notice what happened: "And when the burnt offering began, the song of the LORD also began, with the trumpets and with the instruments of David king of Israel. So all the congregation worshiped, the singers sang, and the trumpeters sounded; all this continued until the burnt offering was finished" (2 Chron. 29:27b–28). As the offering was burning, the nation sang. They had every reason to sing. Their fellowship with God, broken by sin for so many years, was now restored. The altar had been rebuilt, and God was again the object of their worship. They were ready to sing.

The condition of the heart is reflected in whether we even want to sing. The singing of the church in some other parts of the world, especially where the church has been through the fire of persecution, stands in stark contrast to the lack of singing in so much of the North American church. I believe it was A. W. Tozer who once said that if anyone did not desire to worship God down here, they were not ready for heaven.

Notice what happened next. "And when they had finished offering, the king and all who were present with him bowed and worshiped. Moreover King Hezekiah and the leaders commanded the Levites to sing praise to the LORD with the words of David and of Asaph the seer. So they sang praises with gladness, and *they bowed their heads and worshiped*" (vv. 29–30, italics added).

In light of these examples of returning to corporate worship, let me pose several questions. Is there debris that needs to be removed from the corporate life of your church before acceptable worship can be offered? Have you or your church become satisfied with substitutes for the reality of God's presence in your worship services? Are you spending more time in *pumping up* than in *praying down*? Have you or your church lost your song? Christians who do not have a song or who do not desire to worship have a heart problem. Does the altar of prayer need to be rebuilt in your own life or in the life of your church? God help us as His people to be as ready and willing as King Hezekiah and Asa to take whatever steps are necessary to become a people of whom it will be said: "Surely God is in their midst."

Choir Covenant

In applying for membership in our Church Choir[1], we wish you to be fully acquainted with the spiritual and practical implications of such an important share in the worship of God. Experience has proved that the influence of a Choir can never be neutral, and that the whole spiritual life of the church is affected by the condition of the Choir. We want you, therefore, to give prayerful consideration to the terms of the "Covenant of Membership," and then append your signature and return it to the Pastor before being received into the membership of the Choir.

1. I hereby give witness to the fact that I have received the Lord Jesus Christ as my personal Savior, and acknowledge His authority to rule my life by the power of the Holy Spirit.
2. I appreciate the importance and significance of my membership in the Church Choir and will therefore endeavor to relate my interest and work in the Choir to the rest of the life of the church.
3. I recognize that failure to comply with the terms of this covenant will call for such discipline as may be deemed necessary by action of the church.
4. I agree to submit my voice to such evaluation as the Music Director may require, and to accept his decision as to my suitability for the Choir as final.
5. I promise to be regular in attendance at Choir rehearsal, and to give loyal support to the Music Director and to all the ministry of the Choir.
6. I acknowledge that the testimony of my lips should be the outward expression of my Christian experience and that, therefore, holiness of character and conduct should characterize my life at all times.

7. I understand that although I am leading the worship of the church in song, I must be inconspicuous in so doing and that my whole aim must not be to attract attention to myself, but rather by my Christian behavior and humility seek to point people to the Lord Jesus Christ. My ambition must be to sing every anthem, solo, or hymn with the definite object of magnifying my Lord and bringing blessing to those who watch and listen.

8. I realize that every service in the church constitutes a spiritual conflict between the forces of heaven and hell, and that the enemy of souls will always seek to oppose the work of conversion and blessing. Knowing this, I shall endeavor by a constant spirit of prayerfulness and expectancy to share the burden of the ministry with the Pastor.

Having carefully and prayerfully read the conditions and implications of Choir membership, I gladly assent to them and trust by the power of the Holy Spirit to adhere to them.

Signature   _____

Date   _____

Checklist for Worship Leaders

PASTOR:

1. Has the worship team spent sufficient time in planning and praying *together* for the service?

2. Are we of one heart and mind? Is there anything that would hinder God's blessing us?

3. Is the service we have planned man-focused or God-focused?

4. Do I know what is planned during the pre-service time to prepare the people's hearts to worship?

5. Will the people have the opportunity to express themselves in worship, other than when they sing? Is anyone reading Scripture? Will there be a time for them to pray? Will there be an opportunity for anyone to give testimony to the grace of God in their lives?

6. Do I know the message of the special music that will be sung before I get up to preach? How will I bridge from the music to my message?

7. Have I given sufficient thought to what and how I am going to pray: the Scriptures I will use, the thanksgiving and praise I will offer, and the petitions I will make?

8. Am I planning to say anything that would grieve the Holy Spirit? Am I planning to tell a joke when I stand to preach the Holy Word of God?

9. Am I ready to apply the message I will preach to my own life?

10. Am I myself ready to worship?

DIRECTOR OF MUSIC:

1. Are my mind and heart in tune with the pastor's? Have we spent time together to plan and pray for the worship service? Does the pastor know what I will be doing?

2. Is the music I will be using in the service primarily person-focused or God-focused?

3. Am I giving the congregation the words in song that they need to say to God in order for them to worship Him?

4. Is the music I will be using more conducive to worship or to celebration?

5. Is there some Scripture I might use to make the congregational singing or special music more meaningful?

6. Do I know what the soloist is going to sing? Will the music and message cause the congregation to think greatly of God or of the soloist?

7. Am I prepared, along with the pastor, to help the people respond to the special music in a God-focused way and not simply let them applaud everything?

8. Is the pre-service music I am planning conducive to helping the congregation prepare their hearts for true worship?

9. Does the invitation hymn give the people the words they need in order to respond to what God will have said to them through the message?

10. Am I myself ready to worship?

On Preparation for the Lord's Supper

Twenty-Four Questions to Ask Yourself

(from a mid-1800s article in the Georgia Baptist *Christian Index*)

1. In the interval since last partaking of the Lord's Supper, what progress have you been making in your Christian life in proportion to the blessings of God you enjoy? Are you really gaining ground?

2. Is your soul actually strengthened and refreshed?

3. Are your corruptions growing weaker, and your graces growing stronger?

4. Are you able more successfully to strive against your besetting sin?

5. Is your love for the Savior deepening in your heart, and more influential in your life?

6. Is your conformity to His image more distinctly visible to the eye, both of God and man?

7. Are you advancing in love and charity to all men?

8. Do you find that since your last commemoration of this feast of love, you have become so much more full of the Holy Spirit, that you cannot only freely forgive from your heart the most unprovoked and aggravated injuries and insults, but you delight in pouring out fervent prayer on behalf of your bitterest enemy and are ready to minister to his temporal and eternal welfare?

9. Have you felt a warmer interest in the welfare of all who come under your influence?

10. Are you treading more closely in the steps of Him who went about doing good to the bodies and souls of men?

11. Have you expended more time and money in acts of practical benevolence to alleviate the wretchedness, and contribute to the enjoyment, both temporal and spiritual, of those whom it is in your power to help?

12. Are you more gentle and affectionate in your manners at home?

13. Are you more consistent in your endeavor to lead to Christ those you know who have not yet met Him, and to lead those who do know Him into a closer walk with Him?

14. Do you have a growing interest in ministries that labor to promote the glory of God?

15. Can you testify that you are denying yourself the excesses of luxury, whether in dress or any other department, in order to support the Lord's work and thus become a benefactor, in the highest sense of the word, to your family, church, friends, country, and all mankind?

Ask yourself also such questions as the following, in your self-examination.

16. Am I advancing in the joys and comforts of the Holy Spirit?

17. Since I last partook of the Lord's Supper, have I more faithfully followed the promptings of the Holy Spirit; have I listened more teachably to the slightest whisperings of His voice; have I cherished more carefully His sanctifying influences; have I guarded more jealously against the indulgence of any thought or desire that would grieve Him, or cause Him to have to withdraw, even for a season, the manifestations of His love and the communications of His grace?

18. Have I a sweeter sense of my Redeemer's love?

19. Do I find communion with Him a foretaste of heaven?

20. Do I look forward with increasing desire for the day when I shall sit down with Him at the marriage supper of the Lamb?

21. Do I find increasing happiness in meditating on His love when I am alone; in talking about Him when I am with other Christians, and pleading His cause with those who don't know the preciousness of His name?

22. Since I last commemorated His dying love, do I have a larger measure of gratitude towards Him, that caused the pardoned penitent of old to bathe His feet with her tears, to wipe them with the hairs of her head, and pour upon them the most precious ointment she could afford to purchase, as a token of the gratitude with which her heart overflowed?

23. Do I increasingly feel it to be my highest privilege and happiness to lavish on Him every manifestation of my love; to consecrate to Him whatever I possess most precious; every gift He has bestowed, every talent He has entrusted to me; and to esteem myself honored, with the highest honor that any created being can enjoy, in being permitted to be an instrument in advancing His cause, and promoting His glory?

24. Am I continually realizing so much more of the blessed mind of Christ, that I am able to fully enter into the spirit of that sweet hymn which breathed such love to Jesus, while contemplating Calvary's cross, the kind of love that ought to be perpetually burning on the altar of every believer's heart, and that brings down the very essence of heaven's joy into the believer's soul?

APPENDIX 4

When Church Was Just Church[1]

Worship Center or Theater?

———————◆———————

"Do you remember when church was just church?" she asked. Her question caught me by surprise. I wasn't exactly sure what she was asking until she went on to say, "I sometimes feel as though I'm attending a show. I have season tickets to the college theater and concert series and find that the atmosphere there is not much different than it is at my church. Our church productions are just as good, though, and the tickets are cheaper." She smiled as she said that, but I noted a concern in her voice and perhaps a bit of nostalgia. What was she saying? Was she talking about the "good old days" that usually were not quite as good as we remember them to be, or was she describing a genuine problem we face today? Though I may not be able to go back as far as some, I do remember when what happened "in church" looked different, sounded different, *was* different than the world. I don't remember a perfect church, but I do remember *when church was church.*

Perhaps we need to go back to our beginnings and rediscover our roots. It probably wouldn't hurt for any of us to lay aside the books of men for a while and just read what the Bible has to say about the church. We need to take a good look at ourselves and begin asking questions like: why, with all our new and creative approaches, are we having such little impact on the world around us?

Might it be said that the infant church of the first century was more powerful in its witness, more consistent in its faith, and more majestic in its simplicity than today's church with all its sophistication, advanced knowledge, mechanics, programs, props, and footlights? Is that because today's world is very different than it was back then, or is it possible that we have forgotten who we really are supposed to be? Have we lost sight of what the church really is? Could it be that the world has so pressed us into its way of thinking and operating that we're not that much different from them in our lifestyle of promotion and production?

The affluence of the Western world has made it possible for many of our congregations to build expensive buildings. We call these buildings "churches," though actually the building is not the church—the people are. In some cases these buildings rival anything the world can build. Though the Lord indicated that the places where His people meet would be places of prayer and worship, these days we are often more prone to design *auditoriums for audiences* rather than *worship centers for worshipers*. Many of these auditoriums are built more for production than participation; more for theater than worship.

Why are we doing this? Could it be that we now perceive the meeting place to be more of a theater, where actors onstage perform for an audience, than a place for worshipers to offer God their adoration and praise, to bring their offerings and make their prayers?

EVEN OUR ACOUSTICS SPEAK

Our approach to acoustics supports this. We think less of the acoustical properties that are necessary to help and encourage the congregation in its worship than we do of providing the comfort and aesthetic pleasure of carpets, padded seats, and drapes for an *audience* of listeners. The deliberate acoustical design of the room is not planned to enhance the natural sound of worshiping voices, but the amplified sound of those "onstage." So it is that the audience hears the performers well, while barely hearing one another worship. Today the rule of thumb seems to be accommodating our acoustics to sound systems rather than providing the best acoustical ambiance for a worshiping congregation.

For years I led choir ministry tours to Europe. How often have I heard choir members comment on how much better they sounded in Europe than they did back home! In actuality, the only difference was in the acoustics of the churches in which they were singing. They had never really heard their natural God-given voices. They had only heard themselves through manmade monitors. The very expressions on their faces changed as they sang on tour. What a shame. But think of our congregations as they sing. They don't even have monitors! And we wonder why our people don't sing better? The very structure of our buildings discourages congregational participation.

FROM WORSHIP PLATFORM TO THEATER STAGE

"Solomon had made a bronze platform five cubits long, five cubits wide, and three cubits high, and he had set it in the midst of the court; and he stood on it, knelt down on his knees before all the assembly of Israel, and spread out his hands toward heaven" (2 Chron. 6:13).

My use of the word *stage* is deliberate, for even the terminology of today is symptomatic of how far we have strayed from what the Bible says we are. Having traveled for over thirty years in ministry, most of it in the area of music, we have seen many changes. We've watched and listened as church vocabulary has evolved. Some of it has been the natural addition of words to include all the new electronic equipment and gadgets that are now a part of our world. Other changes, however, reveal a disturbingly different attitude toward worship. I'm hearing the words *stage* and *audience* being used more and more. I'm hearing about spotlights and footlights, of backdrops and scrims. I'm hearing the vocabulary of the theater.

We recently held an *Experiencing God in Revival* conference in a rather large church in the south. The minister of music phoned me prior to the first meeting to see what our needs would be. He described the "stage." He asked whether we would like the piano to be located on stage left or stage right. It had been so long since I had done any theater that I wasn't sure *what* I wanted. He then asked what kind of lighting I would like to have highlight us when we sang. I said I wanted it to be just like a church service. He said that they always dimmed the lights in the "auditorium" and spotlighted whoever was "performing" on stage. I said I really didn't want any dimming or spot-lighting, but would rather leave all the lights up. There was then the choice of microphones, whether we wanted reverb added to the voice and so on. I was soon to discover that the choir rehearsal room was called the music theater. I had the feeling that we were going to a concert hall. What was supposed to be the church sanctuary or worship center was more like a huge theater. If it were not for the baptistry (this was a Baptist church), one would not have been able to tell the difference. I counted in excess of one hundred forty theater lights of one sort or another trained on the stage. It all seemed to focus on production and entertainment.

Some time ago I attended a music conference where a minister of music told of the tremendous help he was getting from such entertainment industries as Disney World. The conferees discussed at length the new theater paraphernalia that was now available to enhance their productions and make them look like the real thing. "Absolutely astounding what can be done today" was the consensus. Without realizing it, the church has embraced what the world has been doing for years. The world doesn't know the real and has to create a substitute. They call it "virtual reality." What does this term mean?

Virtual means appearing to be real, when in fact, it isn't. *Reality* means the quality or state of being real; what actually exists, not pretended. So what we have is real unreality; or is it unreal reality?

THE CHRISTIAN WORLD OF VIRTUAL REALITY

I was stretched out on the floor, having just returned from an early-morning run. I'd pushed my body a little harder than usual, and I was now experiencing the "reality" of pain. My muscles were reacting and I felt every ache. I flipped on the TV to a religious channel just as the host was describing what he called "one of the most exciting new phases of our ministry: a Virtual Reality Theater. It's a place where your people can go and experience as close to the real thing as is humanly possible," he said. "We've recreated the Big Bang. You'll be there at creation when God says, 'Let there be light.' You'll be with the shepherds at the annunciation of Jesus' birth. You'll follow them to the manger. You'll be at the Jordan River when John baptizes our Lord. It's just as though it were real." *Just as though it were real?*

We live in "the age of virtual reality." We live in a synthetic world. We live in a world of substitutes. We have substitutes for just about everything, and the substitutes look, feel, taste and sound so much like the real thing that we just accept them as real. Man has become a pro at replacing the real. And the more accustomed we get to our substitutes, the more disoriented we become to what is real. This presents no problem in many areas of life, but when it comes to the things of the Spirit, *there are no substitutes. God does not accept substitutes.*

When did all this start? Is it God's will for the church to be in the virtual reality business? At what point, and to whom, did the Lord say that His house of prayer was no longer to be simply a place to pray, worship, preach, and fellowship? At what point did the Holy Spirit indicate that He needed more than the preaching of Scripture, prayer, and faithful witness to bring people to repentance? Has the real become so unreal and uninteresting to Christians today that we have to provide virtual reality substitutes? Is that what we have to do to keep even our own members interested in going to church?

The Church and Entertainment

We live in an entertainment-crazed world. In many ways the spirit of this age has entered the church, not through the back door but through the front. Not only have many of our buildings become theaters, but many in the ministry are acting more and more like performers onstage. The simplicity of the gospel message and the purity of true worship are being overshadowed by the glitz of showmanship. This is not only true in the field of music, but also in preaching. *Today God often is used to display man's talent rather than man's talent to display God.* And this is happening right before our eyes, "in church." What place does entertainment have in the context of a worshiping church?

There may be times when Christians feel God leading them to be on mission with Him in the lighting and salting of the entertainment world. We could list examples of those who have lived uncompromising lives and have effectively honored God in very difficult circumstances. For them, this is a call to a mission field. But is *the church* a place for entertainment? If not, what is the church doing in the theater business? Today, however, if you work it right, you have the choice of being an entertainer in the world *and* in the church. And as far as the thrill of applause and the glory of moments in the limelight, those can now be found as much in church as in the world.

Worship Is All Eyes on Jesus

"Ascribe to the LORD, O mighty ones, ascribe to the LORD glory and strength. Ascribe to the LORD the glory due His name; worship the LORD in the splendor of His holiness" (Ps. 29:1–2).

"Praise be to You, O LORD, God of our father Israel, from everlasting to everlasting. Yours, O LORD is the greatness and the power and the glory and the majesty and the splendor, for everything in heaven and earth is Yours. Yours, O LORD, is the kingdom; you are exalted as head over all. Wealth and honor come from You; you are the ruler of all things. In your hands are strength and power to exalt and give strength to all. Now, our God, we give you thanks, and praise your glorious name" (1 Chron. 29:10b–13 NIV).

In Revelation 4–5, we have the record of what the apostle John saw when the heavens were opened and he observed the worship of the Lamb. Can you imagine any one of the four living creatures or twenty-four elders maneuvering in order to get some of the glory directed their way? Can you imagine them doing anything to attract attention to themselves? Worship is *all eyes on Jesus!* Even the Holy Spirit, the very Spirit of the Godhead, the Spirit of truth, "will testify of Me," said Jesus (John 15:26). His mission is to lead us into all truth and point everyone to the Lord Jesus. Whenever we seek the applause of man or crave the "spotlight" for ourselves in the name of Jesus, we are robbing God of what is exclusively His—*His Glory*. "I am the LORD . . . My glory I will not give to another" (Isa. 42:8).

It matters not if the world has heard or approves or understands. The only applause we are meant to seek is the applause of nail-scarred hands.

Have you been called to serve
where others tried and failed?
But with God's help and strength
your efforts have prevailed?
Touch not the glory!

Have you some special gift,
some riches you can share,
Or are you called of God
to intercessory prayer?
Touch not the glory!

Has God appointed you
to some great noble cause,
Or put you where you hear
the sound of men's applause?
Touch not the glory!

> A watching world still waits
> to see what can be done
> Through one who touches not
> that which is God's alone.
> Touch not the glory
> for it belongs to God.[2]

Should this not be a concern? The promotion and hype, the glitz and glitter, of a lot of today's gospel ministry has been replacing God's glory. Rather than admitting that His presence is no longer with us, we pull out more gold and silver paint. We paste on more sequins. We turn on more colored lights. We crank up the volume. We perfume and perm and add more makeup. We substitute and imitate. We go on with our act and become so accustomed to our "virtual reality" life that we don't miss the Lord. We are not unlike God's people in Jeremiah 2 who exchanged *God's glory, His very presence,* for other gods, and no one even missed Him! They were going on with their substitutes, not realizing that God had departed. "They did not ask, 'Where is the LORD, who brought us up out of Egypt? . . .' The priests did not ask, 'Where is the LORD?' . . . Has a nation ever changed its gods? . . . But my people have exchanged their Glory [God's presence in their midst] for worthless idols. . . . My people have committed two sins: They have forsaken me, the spring of living water, and have dug their own cisterns, broken cisterns that cannot hold water" (Jer. 2:6–13 NIV).

The irony of it all was that they had experienced God's phenomenal provision in the past. But now that their hearts had departed, instead of realizing that something was wrong, they began to think and act more and more like the godless nations around them. We hear God asking them, "Why go to Egypt to drink water from the Shihor? And why go to Assyria to drink water from the [Euphrates] River?" (v. 18 NIV). He was saying, "Why don't you trust Me anymore? Why won't you turn to Me for what you need? Why won't you do it My way?" In verse 27 he says, "They say to wood, 'You are my father,' and to stone, 'You gave me birth'" (NIV). They were bowing down to things they had made. They found more pleasure in their own creations than in God Himself.

Things, objects of wood and stone, can still capture our hearts and imagination and before we know it we are bowing before substitute gods. When Jesus said, "Where your treasure is there will your heart be also," He was saying that we worship what is most important to us. *A church building can be our god.* People are often more ready to talk about their beautiful facility than they are about the things of God. And programs can become more important to us than prayer, despite Jesus' words "My house shall be called a house of prayer" (Matt. 21:13b). We don't have to go any farther than looking at the attendance at our prayer meetings to see that this is true.

It must have been a shock to the church in Sardis (Rev. 3:1) to receive that letter from the Lord through the apostle John. They thought they were doing well. They had a reputation of "being alive." Today, being "alive" would mean good growth, exciting programs, and upbeat worship services. But the Lord said to the church in Sardis, "You are dead." What was wrong? Somewhere along the line they had begun substituting for the "real thing." They had become satisfied with "virtual reality."

> We've grown so accustomed
> to doing things our way
> We haven't missed You, Lord
> when You weren't there.
> We keep the programs going,
> we motivate and plead
> We're good at work,
> but not so good at prayer.
>
> Lord, we've replaced Your glory
> with manmade pageantry.
> We're good at imitating
> wind and fire.
> We try to recreate, Lord,
> what only You can do.
>
> We substitute our programs
> for Your power.
> Lord, we have dug our cisterns
> and tried to keep them full
> With new and better methods
> every day.
> In seeking for success, Lord,
> we'll go to any means,
> Except to seek Your face,
> except to pray.

> There's someone on the outside
> who's knocking at the door,
> It is the Lord, He's wanting
> to come in.
> Does anybody hear Him,
> does anybody care?
> Who will respond
> and open up to Him?
>
> When the Glory's gone,
> will no one wonder why?
> When the Glory's gone,
> who is going to care?
> When the Glory's gone,
> who's going to ask,
> "Where is the Lord?"
> When the Glory's gone,
> when the Glory's gone.[3]

Are there signs of departure from the "main thing" in your church? Have you become satisfied with substitutes? Is an *inordinate* amount of time and money being spent on activities that are dispensable, that are not mandatory to the church being the church? A pastor friend of ours lamented the fact that almost three hundred of his best people were not in prayer meeting because the music program now needed that time as well. Another pastor wondered how many of his people would still be in church if they only had the less glamorous activities of prayer meetings, witnessing, Bible study, and so forth. Let's think about that for a moment.

What if . . . a one-year moratorium were called on all activity that would fall under the category of theater? (I'm not talking about the week-to-week worship ministry of the choir[s].)

What if . . . those *four million* "man-hours" (a conservative estimate) spent annually by the churches in America on planning, practicing, and preparing of sets, costumes, music, and so on, were spent in prayer, witnessing, and reaching out to the physical and spiritual needs of our communities?

"I was hungry and you gave Me food; I was thirsty and you gave Me drink; I was a stranger and you took Me in, I was naked and you clothed Me; I was sick and you visited Me; I was in prison and you came to Me" (Matt. 25:35–36).

What if . . . the more than *one hundred million dollars* spent annually by the churches in America on their theater productions were spent on home and foreign missions? A minister of music once talked to me about the few "lasting" decisions that were made as a result of the megabucks and hours spent on their annual pageant. He said that there was always a lot of momentary excitement and many on-the-spot decisions, but a very small percentage of those people could be found in church a year later.

The apostle Paul talked about things that were permissible but not necessarily expedient or profitable. He told the Corinthian church that though everything might be permissible, not everything is beneficial or constructive (1 Cor. 10:23). In other words, there are things that we *could* do; but when weighed against the expenditure of time and money compared with the end result, we may find them not to be profitable. Those precious hours of our lives of which we are stewards and the tithes and offerings that represent the sacrifices and worship of God's people might be better spent another way. Jesus said: "Therefore go and make disciples of all nations, baptizing them in the name of the Father and of the Son and of the Holy Spirit, and teaching them to obey everything I have commanded you. And surely I am with you always, to the very end of the age" (Matt. 28:19–20).

Several years ago I was to speak at a church convention in the Northwest. They had asked me months before to send the sermon title and Scripture text as they wanted to include these in the program. I had told them I would speak out of Jeremiah 2 and the message would be, "Has Anyone Seen the Lord Lately?"

When I arrived at the convention, the message had not yet really come together, though I basically knew what was on my heart to say. The night before I was to speak I had a dream. In the dream I was attending a pageant being held in a large church sanctuary. Above the congregation were choir members dressed as angels, "flying" around suspended by some kind of mechanical grid. As singers sang about "angels hovering o'er us," the audience watched in rapt attention at this miraculous sight.

Suddenly I noticed a solitary angel far up in the top corner of the sanctuary, watching what was happening. There was something different about this angel and as I looked more closely, I realized that this angel was real. Looking even more closely I saw a puzzled look on his face, and in my dream I knew what he was thinking: "Why are they doing all this when they could experience the real?"

I abruptly awoke. I found my Bible and pad and started to write. I wrote nonstop for over two hours. The whole message came together. The message was about the condition of God's people as illustrated in Jeremiah 2. (I've dealt with that earlier in this appendix.) They had become so satisfied with substitutes that no one missed the presence of God. No one was asking, "Where is the Lord?"

I wonder what the angels of heaven think about our substitutes. I wonder what God thinks when we spend so much time imitating the real instead of seeking the real, instead of seeking His face.

> "If my people, who are called by my name, will humble themselves and pray and seek my face and turn from their wicked ways, then will I hear from heaven and will forgive their sin and will heal their land" (2 Chron. 7:14).

When the manifest presence of God is among His people, those seeking the truth are drawn to the Light by the reality of a living God in the midst of His people.

When we have the real thing, do we need to bring animals into our churches, hang choir members dressed like angels from the ceiling, or use all the latest laser technology to impress the world with the gospel? Is that what we're called to do? Is that what church is?

As God's people, we should always be willing to take time to evaluate what may be giving a false picture to the world, and to our own people, of what Christianity really is. Anything we are not willing to subject to the scrutiny of the Holy Spirit and the plumb line of God's Word is, at the very best, suspect.

What we have been speaking about in this chapter points to how desperately we need revival. We have been influenced by the world more than we realize. We've been thinking like the world. We've been acting like the world. We've been seeking the world's counsel and following the world's lead. The world needs to see the church just *being* the church again! "Then the nations will know that I am the LORD . . . when I show myself holy through you before their eyes" (Ezek. 36:23b NIV).

> Oh God, Oh God, our nation
> needs the Savior,
> It needs to see a church
> alive and well.
> So many, Lord, are bound
> by Satan's stronghold,
> And we've been called
> to storm the gates of hell.
>
> Lord, not for praise of men,
> but for Your glory;
> Lord, not that we might boast,
> but for Your Name.
> Forgive us, cleanse us,
> fill us with Your Spirit,
> Oh Lord, revive Your people
> once again.[4]

"Therefore, I urge you, brothers, in view of God's mercy, to offer your bodies as living sacrifices, holy and pleasing to God—this is your spiritual act of worship. Do not conform any longer to the pattern of this world, but be transformed by the renewing of your mind" (Rom. 12:1–2a).

Endnotes

Part 1

Letter 6

1. Words by Ron Owens from the song "Precious Lord," © 1979 Ron and Patricia Owens.

Letter 8

1. Words by Ron Owens from the song "Try Praising the Lord," © 1979 Ron & Patricia Owens.

Letter 10

1. Words by Erma Davison from the song "Touch Not The Glory," © 1993 Ron and Patricia Owens.

Letter 13

1. Words by Ron Owens from the song "Bend Me Lower," © 1993 by Ron and Patricia Owens.

Letter 14

1. From the song "Anyway, Anytime, Anywhere" by Ron Owens.

2. Words by Ron Owens from the song "God Is Looking for a People," © 1993 Ron and Patricia Owens.

3. Words by Ron Owens from the song "Use Me," © 1983 Ron and Patricia Owens.

Letter 15

1. From "When I Survey the Wondrous Cross."

Part 2

Letter 20

1. Words by Ron Owens from the song "Preach The Word," © 1993 Ron & Patricia Owens; dedicated to Dr. Stephen F. Olford and The Olford Center for Biblical Preaching.

Letter 22

1. Words by Ron Owens from the song "The Stillness of a Silent Sound," © 1993 Ronald J. and Patricia H. Owens.

Letter 24

1. Words by Ron Owens from the song "A Living Sacrifice," © 1997 Ron and Patricia Owens.

Letter 25

1. Words by Ron Owens from the song "New Creation," © 1985 Ron & Patricia Owens.

Letter 28

1. Hank Hannegraaff, *Counterfeit Revival: Unmasking the Truth Behind the World Wide Counterfeit Revival* (Dallas: Word, 1997).

Letter 34

1. From "When I Survey the Wondrous Cross."

Appendixes

Appendix 1

1. Reprinted with permission from Stephen F. Olford and David L. Olford, *Anointed Expository Preaching* (Nashville: Broadman & Holman Publishers, 1998).

Appendix 4

1. © 1996 Fresh Springs, Inc. Used by permission.

2. Words by Erma Davison, used in the song "Touch Not the Glory," © 1993 by Ron and Patricia Owens.

3. Words by Ron Owens, used in the song "When the Glory's Gone," © 1993 by Ron & Patricia Owens.

4. From "Lord, Do It Again," © 1993 by Ron Owens.